# ADVENTURES IN CAMELOT

## HOW ONE WOMAN'S QUEST TO UNDERSTAND HER SON LED TO DISCOVERING HER TRUEST SELF

## DANIELLE GARY

The ideas, suggestions, and strategies shared in this book are not intended as a substitute for seeking professional guidance. If such level of assistance is required, the services of a competent professional should be sought.

## ADVENTURES IN CAMELOT
Copyright © 2023 by Danielle Gary

First paperback edition May 2023
Edited by Shannan Garrison
Cover photo by Kati Maxwell Photography
Cover design by Rob Gary

Grateful acknowledgement is made to the following for permssion to reprint previously published material:
**Alfred Music.** JUST ONE PERSON (from the musical "Snoopy"). Lyrics by HAL HACKADY. Music by LARRY GROSSMAN. © 1976 (Renewed) UNICHAPPELL MUSIC, INC. All Rights Reserved. Used by Permission of ALFRED MUSIC.
**Hal Leonard LLC.** The Scientist. Words and Music by Guy Berryman, Jon Buckland, Will Champion and Chris Martin Copyright © 2002 by Universal Music Publishing MGB Ltd. All Rights in the United States Administered by Universal Music - MGB Songs International Copyright Secured All Rights Reserved Reprinted by Permission of Hal Leonard LLC.
**Penguin Random House LLC.** Excerpt(s) from RISING STRONG: THE RECKONING. THE RUMBLE. THE REVOLUTION. by Brené Brown, copyright © 2015 by Brené Brown, LLC. Used by permission of Spiegel & Grau, an imprint of Random House, a division of Penguin Random House LLC. All rights reserved.
"Our Children, Our Awakeners" from THE AWAKENED FAMILY: A REVOLUTION IN PARENTING by Shefali Tsabary, Ph.D., copyright © 2016 by Shefali Tsabary. Used by permission of Viking Books, an imprint of Penguin Publishing Group, a division of Penguin Random House LLC. All rights reserved.

Library of Congress Cataloging-in-Publication Data available upon request.

ISBN    978-1-0881-0810-9
eISBN    978-1-0881-0818-5

www.daniellegary.com

# ADVENTURES

**For Cameron,**

In my illusion I thought I was going to raise you
To be whole, complete, worthy,
To be educated, kind, and wise,
To be a leader, empowered and free.
I was deluded to think I knew it all,
Fooled by my age and might.
I thought I had it all together,
Ready to teach, inspire, and change you.
Only now, after so many moments
With you
Do I realize how foolish these ideas were,
How baseless and grandiose.
I now understand...
That it is you who is here to teach me,
To guide, lead, shift, and elevate,
To transform, awaken, and inspire
Me.
I now realize how I had it wrong,
Upside down and outside in,
It is you who are this perfectly designed clarion
To wake me up to my true self.

"Our Children - Our Awakeners" from *The Awakened Family: A Revolution in Parenting* by Shefali Tsabary

# PREFACE

Dear Reader,

The book you hold in your hands is the product of countless lessons learned from my life's greatest teacher: my son, Cameron.

Although it will offer you some insight into his world, this story is about *my journey*, not his.

Cam was born in 2010, and our lives have been a beautiful whirlwind of spectacular color and chaos ever since. In 2012, after a profound regression, a developmental pediatrician diagnosed him with autism, and everything we had imagined about our futures changed in an instant. If I'm being honest, it was terrifying. But only at first. The fear came from my ignorance and the feelings of limbo as we tried to determine the best course of action for our son and our little family. This magic formula we sought was ever-elusive—a unicorn, of sorts. Luckily, we had some great people in our village who helped us find our balance.

As you read these chapters, you'll notice each one is a vignette written in real time. The stories within them are my wholehearted truth, exactly as I experienced them. The tense often shifts depending on whether I am in the moment or have just recovered from it. I kept many of the shifts because altering them felt disingenuous, and I feared altering them to the past tense (simply because they happened in the past) was akin to stepping out of the truth. Compiling these journals and social media entries into a book was a great labor of love, mainly because revisiting some stories broke open the parts of me I thought had healed. However, giving life to this book strengthened me in ways I never imagined possible.

There are also many gaps in time that are unaccounted for. It was during these stretches of missing time and untold stories that I was treading water, trying to endure the journey and ensure that my family and my marriage were going to survive as well. The first years of motherhood, a life alongside autism, changing careers, the deaths of my mother and one of my closest friends within a year of each other, followed by the ongoing trauma of COVID, leaving a job and community of "chosen family," whom I love and miss dearly, and finally, moving to New York to pursue the best educational and therapeutic opportunities for our son, were a few of the curve balls that life threw our way.

These stories were significant parts of our journey, but my heart wasn't ready to crack them open yet. During these time gaps, my creativity went into hibernation so that I could move into crisis mode. If I'm being honest, some things were simply too hard to write about, and those tales remain behind clenched teeth, aching to be told. Perhaps one day I will tell them.

Sharing the more extreme details of our fights for appropriate special education services for our son felt like trauma dumping, and I couldn't find a good reason to add to the anxieties of someone who could benefit from this book. I am acutely aware of the feeling of being pushed under the weight of all that we carry. The entire purpose of compiling the stories into this book is to help other parents and caregivers understand that it's going to be okay.

Because it is.

It will be so much more than you ever imagined. You, too, will probably feel as though you're drowning, but there are so many places where you will find inspiration and hope.

As time changes, so do the needs of our son. As the parents of an autistic individual, we've learned to rely not only on the expertise of professionals but also on the wisdom and experiences of the autistic community. We've made mistakes, and we've also made progress, but above all else, we've made a life together that honors who our son is in every way possible. Through trial and error, we discovered Cameron thrives when we take a strengths-based approach to parenting. We've learned through experience that we must always fight for him to receive equitable treatment and a seat at the table. If there isn't one, we have zero qualms about flipping that table. Inclusion and equity aren't optional in our world.

If you're reading this, chances are that you also know and love someone similar to Cam. I hope the vignettes in this book will give you a glimpse into our journey and connect you to what we know to be true: *our lives are full of peaks and valleys*. There are days when the victories are so glorious that we feel invincible and as if we can conquer anything.

Man, there's nothing better than being on those peaks.

We've learned to hang on to that feeling when we find ourselves deep in the valley. When we've lost our footing, we become hopeless, and despair creeps in. It's then that we remember that despair is a liar—we've been atop the peak many times. We hang on for dear life until we're there again. Life in the valley will surely not last forever, although it seems like it is never-ending. This is the ebb and flow of life, though. Because of autism, our lives have become so much more meaningful.

I'm not trying to portray myself as an autism expert. I wholeheartedly believe and hope that I'll always be learning. Luckily, I've found many amazing individuals to guide me in becoming the best advocate and mother that I can be. While this book has an ending, our story does not. I hope that you'll join us for whatever comes next.

♡ Danielle

— · —

# STAR LIGHT, STAR BRIGHT

## OCTOBER 27, 2009

*Star light, star bright,*
*First star I see tonight,*
*I wish I may, I wish I might,*
*Have this wish I wish tonight.*
-Anonymous

F or most of my life, upon seeing that first twinkling in the night sky, I've made a wish. It's quite different from a prayer, mind you. It's reserved for something that you desire that might need to remain between you and the star. No additional work is required; you just throw a wish into the universe.

For the last year, my wishes and prayers have been the same: *please let me have a happy and healthy baby, but above all else, please let me be a good mother.*

I've never been much for desperation, and I'm certainly not one for begging. However, God and I have had some pretty interesting moments this year when I've put it on the line for the Big Guy.

Most recently was the 6 a.m. potty call when I opened my eyes from a deep sleep with two words on my mind: go test! No reason, really. I was due for my period and had become quite used to the rejection each month when the witch would rear her ugly head. Even my husband had gotten used to it. In fact, he hardly said a word these days when I returned from the bathroom with tears streaming down my face, which had become my new monthly ritual now.

I trudged my sleepy self to the bathroom, opened the box, and peed on a stick while praying. Laugh if you want to, but apparently that time of morning is good for the *Heavenly Queue*, when your prayers skip to the front of the line to be heard and amplified. Honestly, I wasn't even done, and the test started flashing. I'll admit that for the first couple of months of trying, I sat and stared down test after test for pathetic amounts of time, willing them to change their result. And unlike the look I reserve for my 7th grade students, the stare-at-the-stick technique was completely ineffective. When I realized it was flashing, I fumbled to remove the stick from the stream and put the cap on. It changed from flashing to *pregnant* in all of about 2.2 seconds!

I shouted for my husband, "Honey! I need you to come in here *right now!*"

Poor, poor Rob.

Blissfully still asleep, he jumped out of bed as I hollered at him from the bathroom. He stumbled in, where I handed him his glasses and the stick.

He looked at me.
He looked at the stick.
He looked at me.
He looked at the stick.

Back and forth, back and forth, and then he whispered, "Oh, my gosh."

We stared at each other until tears began streaming down my face (possibly his too, but I couldn't tell because I couldn't see anything), and then he gave me the most incredible embrace I've ever experienced.

This chapter of our lives seemed so long, but I know it was nothing compared to what some people have to endure in their struggles with fertility. Rob and I were over the moon, and everyone who loved us came along for the ride.

Welcome to our journey!

— • —

# Whoa, Nelly!

## November 22, 2009

I decided months ago that I would be one of those lucky women who never experienced morning sickness.

Throughout my life, I've heard so many women claim they loved every moment of their pregnancy, and I was bound and determined to be just like them!

Unfortunately, my hormones had other plans for me.

Starting on my birthday, of all days, feelings of nausea arrived and settled in for the long haul. All of those glowing pregnant women who raved about the beauty and joy of pregnancy instantly became my nemeses. I knew every pregnancy was unique, but I did not realize my days would start with vertigo and end with me hugging the toilet in tears. My increased superpowers of smell could pick up a Sharpie pen being used in a room down the hall. Anything offensive to the olfactory senses, and my sniffer found it. Add the ever-increasing gag reflexes, which, of course, became directly in tune with the scents of yuckiness. Gross. Did I mention I was a middle school teacher?

To those women who loved every minute of being pregnant, I don't believe you for a second! Pregnancy is a rite of passage. Those glowing women laugh at your trials and shake their heads in unison, as if they've uncovered unspoken secrets because they've survived some sort of war. Only they have! A war of hormones they swear will pass around weeks 12–14, and I'm only halfway there.

In other news, we had our first ultrasound! After waiting to see the doctor, who was in the process of an emergency delivery, the nurse ushered us into a room, where we waited some more. The waiting brought out my old friend, anxiety, and my thoughts spiraled. *There's something wrong, and they're trying to figure out how to tell me. Maybe it was a horrible mistake, and I'm not pregnant! Could that be possible?*

Before too much mania set in, the doctor came in to confirm the urine test showed I was indeed pregnant, and then she said, "Let's take a peek!"

I can't describe the intensity of emotion I felt seeing our child, which, coincidentally, Rob has nicknamed *Junebug*. Although it appeared bean-sized on the screen, the doctor zoomed in so we could have a proper look at the life inside. Sure enough, there was a flickering of a heartbeat, which caught my breath and my heart all at once. The monitor picked it up as a tiny blip, and we watched it travel across the screen.

A miracle.

Our miracle.

It's amazing how quickly some people become relaxed after seeing their baby for the first time. Even though my body was taking care of business, I found it difficult to sit back and let it do its job. Giving up control has never been easy for me, but for this baby, I was ready to try.

# Lil' Junebug

## December 12, 2009

Seeing the baby for the first time at my 7-week checkup was intense, even though all we saw was a bean and a flicker. I think it must be a maternal thing that you can so easily identify with the shapes and movements. However, this did nothing to prepare me for our next visit at 11 weeks. It was as if the earth opened up and swallowed everything I thought I knew about the world. Head, belly, bottom, legs, arms, and a strong heartbeat. Junebug had her little fist up to her face, and when she moved it, I was relieved that it was her hand and not a humongous nose! But then she (we don't know that it is a girl; it just sounds better than "it") moved her little arms, and the picture was so clear. That precious and tiny shape was *our* baby. I was in the loveliest shock and looked to Rob to find some sort of stabilization, but his face was mirroring mine.

In awe.

In love.

For a moment, everything was right in the world. I'd never seen my husband so happy, and I'd never loved that man more than in that very instant.

My dear friend Laura pointed out, "Throwing up today will feel so much more worth it than yesterday!" And she was right.

— • —

# READY OR NOT

## JUNE 9, 2010

R eady or not, here he comes! My pregnancy became high-risk with the diagnosis of oligohydramnios, which is when your amniotic fluid levels dip lower than normal. I spent weeks drinking unfathomable amounts of water and restricting movement as much as possible. Which was kind of funny because all I did those days was waddle to and from the bathroom. After two months of bed rest and constant monitoring, my levels finally entered the danger zone. Baby Cameron (we decided on a name!) has baked for 37 weeks today, and tomorrow we will begin an induction to bring him safely into the world.

Par for the course, this, too, turned out to be the exact opposite of our original plan...

Here we go!

---·---

## SADNESS IN THE MIDST OF OUR GREATEST JOY

### JULY 8, 2010

When we embarked on this journey together, Rob and I knew it would be an adjustment for our family. Not only would the two of us grow into a family of three, but we also had our furry family of two cats, Harley and Diesel, and one dog, Coda, to consider. What we didn't imagine were the intense changes that might come from adding one member to our flock.

Cameron's birth did not go according to plan, and boy, I had entire blueprints! Naively, I had created a dreamy birth plan, starting with which drugs I would allow and ending with details pertaining to cord clamping. Looking back, I realize that this was my way of trying to gain some control over what was going to be the most momentous occasion of my life.

What I had envisioned as a smooth sail into motherhood was actually quite traumatic. Both Cameron and I earned an extended stay in the hospital. Cameron suffered some bruising during birth as he got impossibly stuck in my pelvis upon his exit. This led to some serious jaundice, so he spent the next two days under the bili lights, and we could only hold him every three hours for thirty minutes to feed him. It was torture, only nurturing him with a gentle hand while he lay under the lights and I struggled to recover from severe postpartum anemia. I lost quite a bit of blood during the cesarean section when they had to maneuver Cameron out of his "rock and a hard place" positioning. My extended stay at this all-inclusive resort included two separate blood transfusions, a series of hefty antibiotics, and constant IV fluids.

My memories are hazy when I try to recall those first moments with Cam. I remember the moments after they delivered him and the flurry of the doctors and nurses in the operating room; the silence was deafening. My heart was beating so loudly in my ears, and I was colder than I'd ever been, which frightened me. I remember thinking, *Is this what dying is like? Am I dying?* I looked to Rob, who was beside me on our side of the curtain, which separated us from the doctors and nurses who were at work.

"Please tell me a story—something magical with a happy ending." He put his face close to mine and whispered a story to fill in the space that was occupied by the silence and our fear.

And then I heard Cameron's first cry! My entire body felt it—connected to the deepest, most sacred parts of myself. I sobbed, and at that moment, I had never felt so alive. The nurses brought him over so that we could see his sweet face, and then the world went dark. The next thing I remembered was waking up in the middle of the night, still shaking from the anesthesia. I heard the softest quivering noise nearby, and I turned my head to see my baby boy shivering in an incubator next to me. But then it was lights out again.

The next morning, I spiked a fever of 103.1, which caused a flurry of activity among the hospital staff. They couldn't pinpoint the source of the problem, and I have to admit that for a while I was expecting Dr. House to walk in the door and diagnose me with some obscure condition. After a few scary moments over the next week, they released us once my fever remained at bay.

We arrived home with the highest expectations of rest and a return to normalcy—everyone who has ever been in a hospital knows that there isn't any rest to be found there. However, life had a very different plan for us.

Let's go back about a year. We had been training Coda, our rescue dog, to relax among strangers, as he had a significant amount of fearful aggression. We rescued him from a Los Angeles pound, where he was on his *last day* at only a few months old. Scheduled to be euthanized at 5 p.m., we got there at 9 a.m. to save him. Los Angeles County Animal Control had seized

Coda from a puppy mill in a section of the city known for dog fights, and he was one of nearly 40 puppies that were "rescued." He was a sketchy little guy who didn't know what to do with a toy for weeks. He spent most of his young life in a cement box at the pound, and he was afraid of just about everything.

It was clear from day one that he was a special case, and we worked to help him have a happy life, one that he would not have experienced otherwise.

Coda has remained a special case ever since. He was fearful of most people, but incredibly loving toward his family. Professional training with clickers (positive reinforcement) allowed us to make significant progress with his aggression and his comfort level among strangers. He learned so many tricks and developed a love for learning that was easy to see. As soon as the treat bag came out, he was fully engaged. With our small successes, we hoped it would be a successful transition at our house when we brought the baby home. Rob and I started researching the best methods of introducing the baby, and we followed the advice of our trainers to make our transition smooth. We did everything by the book. What we were not counting on was Coda's reaction being biologically out of his control.

Upon arriving home, we had a very controlled introduction of Cameron to Coda. There was distance, and plenty of attention paid to Coda because we had been gone for many days. He was loving and very excited to see us. However, when he saw the baby, his reaction became intense, with shackles raised and a low and intimidating growl. His aggressive behavior took control, and he concentrated on the baby like a dog that had just seen a squirrel in the garden. His response revealed to us, painfully, that although he was a loving companion to Rob and me, he would not be safe for our new son.

Our trainer had advised us that this was a possibility. We knew it wasn't a safe situation for Cameron and that Coda couldn't control his own reaction. After consulting with her, we resigned ourselves to the fact that Coda's biology was getting the better of him.

As a parent, you must make tough decisions quickly, especially if there is a potential danger to your child. It's an instinct, and only the safety of your little one matters. The moments that followed were devastating. Rob and I placed Coda in a trusted foster situation until we could find him a forever home. For a thousand reasons, our hearts were breaking, and they continued to break for some time. Coda was a terrific dog with a few challenges. He was a loyal and loving companion for almost five years, but he simply couldn't be in a situation with an infant or small children.

*Update: Coda found his forever home with one of our beloved trainers. He joined her pack of several dogs out in the country, where he lived a happy and full life. Looking back, we know we made the best decision for both Coda and our family.*

*Still, sometimes the right choice is the most painful.*

# AND WE'RE BACK!

## JUNE 20, 2011

S omehow, time moved at a different speed in those first days, weeks, and months. To be fair to myself, that time frame coincided with the Texas standardized tests from hell and the end of the school year. Not to mention that in those same 3 months I joined a very intensive physical fitness group, "The Busy Women's Bootcamp," in which I got my ever-loving arse kicked weekly by a personal trainer who is fitter than the fittest fiddle.

You may ask why I subjected myself to this torture.

I wanted to become a healthier mother for my son.

I wanted to not feel anxious and tired all the time. Of course, sleeping through the night would be a *great* start.

I began walking Cam in a stroller three mornings a week.

I doubled my record for push-ups. I did ridiculous stair-climbing workouts in 95-degree heat. I nearly tossed up a protein shake. I went all sparkly in my right eye from exertion. *That's* out of shape!

I ran my first 5K and survived. It was indeed a miracle because my brain was telling me the entire time that I couldn't do it; just slow down and give up if it's too much. I didn't quit, but I came in dead last, and I felt terrific about it!

Cameron turned 1 this month. ONE! An entire year has flashed by in the blink of an eye. I've been so immersed in learning this new role as *Mama* that I didn't even fill out his baby book!

Our amazing little boy is growing like a weed. He is likely to become tall like his dad, as he's already 31 inches long. After his first birthday party, I had a fleeting feeling of sadness that my family wasn't there for the celebration—they live 1700 miles away. Rather than feel sad for what was missing, I embraced the fact that my closest friends and my husband's family were there to celebrate with us. I felt truly blessed in many ways. As a friend once told me, "It takes a village to raise a child. You can build his village."

And so I have. Looking over the pictures from his party, I'd say that we've chosen well. My son is loved dearly.

— · —

# Searching for My Om at Home

August 5, 2011

My mind never stops. I know—no one's mind ever truly stops until they're dead. Well, my mind refuses to give me any sort of rest or reprieve from the constant chaos. Although, as an adult, it is utterly exhausting, I'm sure it is some sort of developmental strategy or coping mechanism that resulted from a childhood that was chaotic at every turn.

I fall asleep, and I have the most lucid and vibrant dreams! The problem is that sometimes I dream so much that I wake up feeling more tired than I was when I went to sleep. I'm not sure that I ever enter that deep, sacred, rejuvenating level of sleep. Heck, I only dream about it. In the past, I've found peaceful rest while practicing yoga. Oh, the blessed savasana! How I love you. This new mama will even take a child's pose for a few moments if it will give me back my center.

During my waking hours, I am a subconscious planner. On the outside, I'm changing the baby, picking up toys, washing the dishes, teaching a class, etc. But inside my mind, the committee behind the curtain is planning for every probable scenario that might occur. They never stop creating contingency plans. They're passing judgment on the driver who cut across the lane without turning his blinker on. They're filing away ideas for home improvement, organization, potential date nights with the husband, which elicit a list of potential babysitters, and so on.

I used to pride myself on my natural ability to multitask, but now I'm simply starving for some peace.

# THE BEGINNING OF THE END OF THE NOISE

## AUGUST 7, 2011

Throughout my life, my mind has been in constant conflict with its own noise. One of the few things that seemed to provide a brief respite was yoga, a tool that I added to my toolbox in 1999. It seemed only natural that I should turn to meditation to quiet the chaos. I'd researched the many benefits of meditation, and everything about the practice really appealed to me. Buddhist philosophy seemed to go hand in hand with the way I wanted to live my life. So, off we went (of course, I dragged my beloved along with me on the first guided meditation adventure!) to the Austin Shambhala Center for an introductory class on meditation.

Upon entering the building, I was immediately at ease. A lovely woman greeted us and brought us into a seated area where other newbies were discussing what brought them to the center.

*Full disclosure: a tiny part of me was afraid that I was going to be immersed in what some call "hippy-dippy bullshit" or something akin to a Scientology nightmare I once had. It couldn't have been further from the truth.*

Some people found the center merely by googling "meditation in Austin." Others had heard about it through friends, acquaintances, etc. One guy was there because his world religions professor had given his class a target list of places to experience. Everyone in the room had a purpose, whether it was seeking a sense of serenity or finishing their last college history course.

They brought us into the meditation room, which looked much like many yoga studios that I have practiced in, with the decor focused on Tibetan art. It was a peaceful room lined with about five columns and six rows of meditation cushions. A gentle soul greeted us and delivered the most relaxing and comfortable instructions I have ever received. As an educator, I attend many meetings and professional development sessions where other educators frantically cram too much information into the minimal time they've got. I thought more than once, *I wish meditation instructors led our work meetings!*

I sat down on a cushion and began my first attempt at meditation. As the instructor suggested, I focused on my breath as the anchor.

I breathed in...

I breathed out...

Hunger pangs strike! Followed by, *I wonder what we're going to have for dinner.*

Back to the breath, Danielle.

Ok, ok, I'm breathing. In... Out... I held a soft focus on my breath, as instructed, and my eyes were gazing softly at the patterns of the hardwood floor in front of me. Breathing in... Breathing out... I concentrated on my breath until I felt myself relax and let go.

Then the most remarkable thing happened! As I inhaled, the soft gaze that my eyes had settled into became immersed in a lavender bath. As I exhaled, the lavender color became magenta. This repeated with every inhalation and exhalation for several moments. I wondered, *Am I meditating? Is this what happens?* Then I realized I hadn't blinked for about five minutes. I was probably depriving my eyes of vital lubrication, or maybe my breathing was introducing some much needed oxygen!

Just as I was about to laugh aloud at myself, I remembered where I was and guided myself back to the meditation. It became increasingly easier with each moment, although there was always the ever-present chatter of my executive committee trying to plan or a stray worry coming into my peripheral thoughts. I gently put each passing thought aside, focused, and slowly felt a semblance of peace.

Next, the instructor guided us through the Buddhist practice of walking meditation. Rather than focusing on the breath, you focus on walking. Seemed easy enough. It started out with a few more distractions as the group was walking in a clockwise circle around the room. Of course, the squeaks in the hardwood floor, ambient sounds of nature, and whispering all became less of a distraction as we shuffled along. Concentrating only on the act of walking, I thought to myself, *I can do this.*

As I began focusing on what my body actually does while walking, I noticed the tiniest details of what had previously seemed so mundane! My legs moved rhythmically and with such purpose, yet somehow the movement seemed difficult the more that I thought about it.

*Am I standing straight? Why is my right leg more awkward than my left?*

Focus on the walking.

*I wonder if I should mention this to my chiropractor.*

Back to the walking, Danielle.

Then, as I passed the movement of my ankles, I stopped at my feet.

I have *never* been so acutely aware of how my toes clung to the ground. That was mind-blowing! While focusing on each step, I felt as if I were losing control of the very ground that I was walking on. How was this even possible? I know how to walk! As I rounded the corner of the room, I almost tipped over. I felt as if I were on a tightrope.

I thought to myself, *This is not relaxing or peaceful; I'm about to fall flat on my face.*

*Who is that speaking inside my head?*

Silence.

I relaxed into the walk, with the thought, *I know how to walk. I've been doing it my whole life.*

And just then, as if instinctually, I thought to myself, *Let go, Danielle. Hey, feet... Shhhhh!*

And they did.

# WOULD YOU RATHER BE RIGHT OR HAPPY?

## MARCH 13, 2012

S o often in my life, I feel compelled to fix things. Broken things, rusty things, tattered, torn, and wrinkly things.

When friends come to me for advice, it's hard not to offer a solution because it feeds the problem-solver within me. Most likely, this part of my nature is the reason I am working to become a counselor. I know better than to try to change the people in my life, as it certainly never works. Instead, I adjust my expectations.

Throughout my entire life, I've created an unrealistic set of expectations for myself, and I'm forever trying to live up to them. These expectations often include my career, personal life, the standards that I set for myself as a parent, and those that I strive for as a human being. I don't fool myself into believing that I always live up to them; in fact, I've become the happiest I have ever been merely by acknowledging that I am a work in progress.

I mess up. I try to reflect on and grow from the experience. But that wasn't always the case.

Sometimes I've messed up so irrevocably that I had to destroy any link between whatever it was and myself. Some relationships have gone up in flames because I was too proud or immature at the time to reflect on or understand my part in their demise. I don't regret these stages because they've led me to appreciate the personal growth that I've experienced. Sure, I regret some of my actions, but I try to forgive myself and move on

One of the greatest lessons I have learned is also one of the most subtle. A friend recently asked me, "Is it better to be right or happy?" The question seemed so irrelevant, but I've thought about it repeatedly ever since.

Ego sure holds a lot of meaning for such a small word.

Does our own perception of our self-importance outweigh the value of our personal connections?

One glance at my social media feed could prove that this is undoubtedly true.

Person A states an opinion. Debate arises over the accuracy of that statement, and we load each comment with sarcasm, not a genuine desire to teach or learn.

Person B posts a serene image with a profound quote, and several people are clamoring to be the first person to tell them that the author of the quote is incorrect or a terrible human.

Person C posts about a revelation that they've recently had, and we rush to put them in their place because their revelation is in direct conflict with our own beliefs, Person C's past actions, or someone enjoys making fun of their experience.

Are we so ego-driven that our desire to be right outweighs another person's happiness? And when did tearing someone else down equate to our own happiness through personal vindication?

Why is it so important to be right—to be *more* right than anyone else? To be smarter than anyone else, have more life experiences, and be happier than anyone else? Do we really need to point these things out to feel validated? Maybe for some people, this is fulfilling. And it's perfectly OK when other people need these validations.

What someone else needs may differ vastly from my own needs, but we *are* different, so why should our needs be in sync?

And to be honest, I'm happier not arguing about it.

There are things that hold great value to me (like equity and inclusion), and I will argue their importance until I'm out of breath. However, my beliefs don't hold the same value for everyone else. If what they think or do doesn't harm the world we share or the people that I love, I can let it go. At the end of the day, everyone is trying to do whatever they believe will make them happy.

Who am I to argue with that?

— · —

## ADULT FRIENDSHIPS CAN BE TOUGH

### MARCH 18, 2012

Recently, Rob and I attended an impromptu dinner with a beloved friend of mine who was visiting Austin for SXSW. We met up with Anjali at a local restaurant, talked in high-speed New York fashion, and caught up over a meal. Then we meandered over to a show, where we hung out ever so briefly with another friend, Andrew, who was presenting a huge showcase for about 4,000 music lovers. He was also working, but made it a point to meet up with us and share a few drinks as we laughed at how far we'd all come. Years ago, we worked together as executive assistants at Interscope, and our lives took each of us down different paths, ending with us all living so very far apart in Los Angeles, New York, and Austin. It was a fast night; it was a long and late night, but it was one of the best nights I've had in years.

See, this is how things are done where I'm from. You may not have a lot of time to spend together, but you make the most of it when you do, and you try to do it as often as possible. There's a feeling that no time has passed and an invigorating sense of community just from the encounter. Take my best friend Jenna, for example. She's lived all over the world, and we haven't lived in the same state since college. Yet when we get together—maybe once a year—we pick up right where we left off. Effortlessly.

Yes, in both New York and Los Angeles, we *made* time for our friends so that we could bask in the feeling we got from the connection. Sure, there are always friendships of convenience. You see them at a common hangout locale, and you revel in each other's company until the next time.

But the genuine connection that you get from spending quality time with someone who really understands you is *pure gold*.

I'm not sure if it happened when my son was born or if it started during my pregnancy, but I have felt a significant amount of social isolation in the past few years. Some of my closest friends are also new mothers, and frankly, it's tough finding time to get together regularly. I live thousands of miles away from my lifelong best friends and my family, so the regular drop-ins that were a staple of my youth don't exist. I never thought that I would miss that so intensely.

I've formed friendships with some people I work with. We frequently invent reasons to get together. Girls' Night Out, Bunco, or even Happy Hour are relatively common occasions with the people I work with. Maybe this is just how adult friendships work. I cherish these women and wish I could spend more quality time with them! The precious moments spent among friends are too infrequent amidst the rest of the chaos.

My husband has been one of my very best friends since we met eight years ago. As a matter of fact, I prefer his company over all others. He gets the quirks of my personality that most people do not understand. He appreciates my loud and excited behavior when I'm passionate about something. Many people misinterpret my intensity and New York directness as being "too much." Rob sees my desire to change the world and make it a better place for our son as courageous. Most people label me an idealist. I appreciate our friendship because, otherwise, I've often felt l onely.

It's the familiar comradery that I miss the most—the ability to turn to a friend who already knows your history and your secrets, so you needn't fear the repercussions when you dump all that junk on a new friend.

I yearn for quality time spent with friends, not out of convenience or even the need to solve many of life's constant dramas, but just out of love for one another. Talking about the newest line of H&M over coffee, laughing at a memory of an embarrassing moment we experienced together, sitting on a dock overlooking the bay with drinks in our hands and smiles on our lips. Memories that seemed like they would always be current and commonplace. The lack of these moments in my life has left me feeling pretty melancholy.

Is this typical of adult relationships? Common for new mothers? Do we find ourselves so immersed in our family lives and day-to-day responsibilities that we simply don't have time to spend on our personal relationships? Sure, my time has been sparse since becoming a mother. The many facets of my daily life are often exhausting and mundane. I treasure every minute I get to spend with my two wonderful boys, yet something is still missing. Life as I knew it, pre-motherhood, will never return. I don't regret or resent the "new" life, but like I said, I'm feeling nostalgic for certain aspects of the "old."

Is this the normal progression of friendships made in adulthood? Are our lives too busy to connect at a deeper level, or am I simply expecting too much?

— • —

# The Weight of a Word

## December 9, 2012

*When we least expect it, life sets us a challenge to test our courage and willingness to change; at such a moment, there is no point in pretending that nothing has happened or in saying that we are not ready. The challenge will not wait. Life does not look back. A week is more than enough time for us to decide whether or not to accept our destiny.*
-Paulo Coelho, The Devil and Miss Prym

S ome stories are very hard to tell. The words hang heavily on the tongue, and the heart weighs even more on the soul.

The *telling* might be therapeutic to some, releasing the words that can create a greater sense of understanding for everyone involved.

But what if the act of telling changes everything? Could you ever turn back, away from the truth? Could you change someone's perspective? Would what they see overcome what their brain wants to tell them? Would they see what we see because of the immense love that we share?

Sometimes not telling is a kinder action.

Then again, sometimes you have to see everything else outside of yourself. Sometimes you just throw yourself at the mercy of others and pray that they have your best interests at heart.

This is our journey. It's full of love, pain, and a whole lot of courage. Our journey became a story the minute that I wrote this. The telling of the story is the hardest part.

The choice to become a mother was one of the single most defining moments of my life. There was a certain appeal to being in my 30s and having very limited responsibilities. Yet something more called to me. A part of me wanted to prove to myself, and maybe the world, that I could become a loving and nurturing parent, despite a laundry list of reasons that I had convinced myself were against me. I grew up in your run-of-the-mill dysfunctional family and have spent my entire life waiting for *someone* to get sober. My mother became pregnant with me at the tender age of 15, so we grew up together. Our relationship was tumultuous at best, and while we repeatedly tried to connect to each other, her mental health struggles often got the best of her, and I got the worst.

I'm not one to believe that having a child completes a family. I didn't think that I could love my husband any more than I did the day we were married. The day that our son was born, I thought that my heart would burst with love. It couldn't possibly grow any stronger.

I was wrong.

The day that our son received an autism diagnosis was the kicker. That day, I realized I loved my husband more than I ever imagined was possible. He had saved me from myself on the journey that we were on, and he helped me pick up the pieces when I fell apart.

We had been on an emotional roller coaster for two months, going from speech pathologists to neurologists to developmental pediatricians, collecting data that would shed some light on why our son had experienced such a drastic change over the summer. In what seemed like a moment, he stopped talking, couldn't tolerate being held, and slowly pulled away from us. The change in the level of interaction that we experienced with him was startling.

I don't know if you can imagine what it is like to desperately wish that the word "mama" would once again come out of your child's mouth. I yearned for his sweet voice, watching videos of him saying it on repeat and mentally replaying it over and over in my mind so that I would never forget it.

Something was different, and we were on a mission to figure it out. In the meantime, we called in the big dogs and started working toward what we knew to be true. One of my best friends since college, Katie, is a behavior analyst specializing in autism. What are the chances of *that*?

She flew down and completed the VB-MAPP, which is an assessment tool for children on the autism spectrum that measures their learning, language, and social skill development. Then she started working one on one with Cam as we observed. Cam responded to her interventions immediately, which she shared was not always the case. We soon learned that there was *nothing* typical of our child.

The visible symptoms of autism weren't consistent. On a good day, you'd never guess. On a bad day, you couldn't deny it, as he retreated inside himself, spending his days lining up toys, stacking blocks for hours, and shifting into an emotional explosion over the slightest changes in routine or environment. I remember vividly how desperate I was to attract his attention one afternoon, but he was stuck in a loop of walking around the living room, trailing his tiny fingers along the wall. I felt invisible to the one person I desperately wanted to connect with—my child.

Katie provided integral guidance pertaining to ethical behavior, and what to look for to determine that providers were following our expectations for care. The big guideposts were the providers' qualifications, their professional background, and their proposed treatment plans. Katie cautioned that, when done with fidelity, ABA (applied behavior analysis, an integral therapy for early intervention) isn't about behavior modification but using positive reinforcement to build skills. This was incredibly important to us because we were ready to do whatever was necessary to help Cam become the best version of himself.

We started using ABA *lite* at home, and the words slowly emerged! We would model a word like "milk," using both sign language and verbal communication while providing tons of praise and reinforcement for any approximation of the word. Cam responded to these strategies so quickly, and as his words increased, his frustration decreased. In one weekend, we went from 5 spoken words to 10, and then over 40. In two weeks, we were at 70+ words. Soon, we lost count.

In two months, our brave boy made the kind of progress that most parents take for granted. One day, it was all I could do not to grab the microphone at Target and shout, "Good evening, Target patrons! My son has made a year's worth of progress in verbal development in two months. Carry on!"

I say that we practiced ABA *lite* because, in reality, we were only using discrete trial training with loads of positive reinforcement, and to see a quality behavior analyst in action is to witness a near miracle. They use strategies that are individualized for each child, and they are incredibly effective during early intervention! As an educator, I could see that I had been using a form of this throughout my career and just didn't have a name for it.

I don't know what the formula was for our success with Cam. I know parents who worked just as hard, if not harder, and the results were different. We knew that time was of the essence, so we pushed. Hard. Every outing and novel situation became teachable moments, full of joy and play.

Rob and I started with ABA because we wanted to give our son the tools necessary for him to reach his full potential. It became a goal to break down the wall that had risen between us. Only certified professionals can administer ABA, and we couldn't afford to hire one without insurance coverage. Insurance will only cover ABA for a diagnosis of an autism spectrum disorder, and not all insurance has options for this coverage. In my school district, they did not cover ABA, period. And it wasn't for a lack of trying to educate them about its importance. In response, I was told that "it simply isn't cost-effective."

There was a tragic irony in spending years supporting other children with various disabilities, including autism, only to be denied vital support for my child. Luckily, we had other options through my husband's insurance.

The catharsis that came with obtaining the words we feared most was indescribable. With three words written on a prescription pad, we could get our son the therapy that he needed.

*Autism spectrum disorder.*

Three heavy and daunting words—but only three.

Three words written on a notepad to describe an integral part of the magnificent human that is our son.

Cameron struggles with two aspects of autism: social interaction and verbal communication. The desire is there, which is our greatest gift, but we discovered that his brain works differently in *how* it learns.

So, we learned to accommodate *his* differences and changed the way *we* teach. And then he began coming back to us.

One afternoon, I had fallen apart and was sitting on the bathroom floor in a heap of tears, snot, and tissues. I stood up, looked in the mirror, and told myself that there was no time for denial, no room for self-pity, and that I needed to pull my shit together in order to help him become who he was meant to be.

In that moment, I made the conscious choice to see Cameron for who he is, and I put my emotions in their place. After all, autism is only a small part of who he is.

Sometimes you have to make an intentional choice to do things differently.

Choose to see the child before the exceptionality.

Choose to acknowledge that autism is how his brain operates, and that he is still the same sweet, creative, and silly little boy that he always was.

You don't *have to.*

But *we need you to.*

He needs you to see him before you see his disability. Because if you see him first, you'll see that he's a work of art. He works harder to understand his world than you and I could ever imagine. The hard work that creates such verbal masterpieces as "Daddy," "Mama," "purple," "open door!" and "Ready set go!" or most recently, "I love you!" These may be scripts, but they're a start, and he works tirelessly to deliver them.

These words are precious to us. They tell us to keep pushing on, that the little person we love has something to say, and that we need to listen.

We will do everything within our power to make sure the entire world hears him.

---·---

# ON MOTHERHOOD

## AUGUST 20, 2013

A s I watched all the sentimental social media updates from my friends who recently entered the realm of motherhood, I wrote a letter to myself. I strung together all the words of wisdom that I wish someone had uttered to me during those stages and prayed for the clarity to absorb them.

*Dear Self,*

*Being a mother is one of the most challenging and difficult jobs you will ever have. The learning curve is steep at first, but it's more about finding your footing than learning how to mother. You'll find yourself weighing your needs against the needs of others and trying to fit those needs into an impossible 24-hour day. Please know that you are not responsible for balancing it all.*

*We each do the best we can with what we've got in front of us, and trudge on while occasionally leaning on our closest friends and family. There are things I know to be true, but perhaps intentionally addressing them here will make the concepts stick.*

*Ask for help when you need it.*

*Say no, and say it often.*

*Don't let anyone tell you that your concerns are not valid; they're probably led by your intuition.*

*Your intuition is probably right.*

*Don't judge yourself by other people's parenting skills, and don't judge others by yours. What we see on the surface is often so blurred by our own perspectives that our vision is biased and inaccurate.*

*Take care of yourself. Eat healthy food and get as much sleep as possible. Seriously, when the baby sleeps, you must sleep. Exercise. Take time for yourself, even if it means begging someone to sit with the baby while you sit in silence, staring at the wall.*

*Get off the internet, hang up the phone, and turn off the TV. As much as possible. These first years are so incredibly fleeting that you don't want to miss a thing. Trust me.*

*If you have to work, know that when you are done with your workday and you are speeding home to see your bundle of joy, you are no less valued than a parent with the ability to care for their child at home.*

*If you are caring for your child at home, know that you have a very important job and also need a reprieve here and there. Don't judge yourself based on this decision, either. Again, we're all doing the best that we can for our given situation.*

*No parent is perfect. If you mess up, make a mistake, or forget something important, chances are that life will go on. As a mother, you're going to worry. Incessantly. Try to keep yourself in check by letting go of the things that you have no control over and leaving behind those that have passed. Learn from them and move on with that knowledge.*

*Now that you have taken on this adventure, your truths in life have changed. There is no greater experience. There is no more important and profound legacy that you could leave for this beautiful world. Enjoy every single moment of struggle, anticipation, and joy.*

*You will feel defeated by exhaustion and the neediness of others—after all, you are now "mother," and you will (frequently) cry over these tumultuous emotions and then laugh maniacally as your newborn, infant, toddler, child, adolescent, or teenager looks at you with horrified confusion. Remember that you just created life, and that makes you a mother flippin' goddess. No matter what life throws your way, you've got this.*

# When You've Lost Track of Who You Are

## November 21, 2013

Since the birth of my first and only child three years ago, I realized I had been struggling. I hadn't felt like myself in a very long time, and while I yearned to feel like the *old* me, try as I might, I couldn't find her.

As the major roles in my life changed, so did I.

I started as individual *me* and eventually became *married me*.

While the major components of my personality stayed the same during this transition, I felt somehow changed. Mostly for the better.

When I changed careers from working in the music business to becoming a middle school teacher, it drastically changed many roles in my life.

After becoming a mother, I left any shred of the old me in the dust. My new self was in survival mode, just trying to get by. There was no *me time* in the equation. Not for a lack of wanting it, but because, as a full-time working mama, being the best mother I could possibly be meant sacrificing myself. Looking back, I realize that this was an error, but I didn't have anyone to guide me.

Oh, there were plenty of people to throw me a line like, "You have to take time for yourself!" But very few people threw me a line that was attached to a life preserver. And, for the record, time for yourself as a new mother should come in regular, predictable, and planned doses. These occurrences should be in the mother's best interest and according to her availability. Don't ask or expect a new mother to get up an hour earlier to work out at the gym. Never expect her to give up the sacred sleep that is all too elusive.

As a new mother, I rarely wanted to do anything other than stare at the wall, lie in the bathtub, or wander aimlessly around Target.

My life changed drastically between 2006 and 2010, and I never really allowed myself to pause and appreciate the changes. Between marriage, moving across the country, a major career change, and motherhood, I experienced several of the most stressful events that occur throughout a person's life. One day, I simply woke up and felt like something was amiss. Because it was.

Although I'm pretty liberal in my beliefs, outwardly I became as conservative as the district that I worked for. I guess I was dressing the part rather convincingly. One day a co-worker startled me as she shrieked in surprise, "You have a tattoo? I had no idea!" I was in more shock than her, I promise you. Then it hit me—I had been working in the same building for seven years, and very few people knew who I really was.

Wait. Who I *was.* I thought to myself, *Who am I?*

I repeated this question to my closest friends, dearest relatives, and my sweet husband, hoping to hear something that would explain how I felt. Mostly everyone laughed and replied, *"You're you!"*

I secretly grieved over this feeling of losing myself. It weighed heavily on my heart and eventually led me to seek a counselor who could assist me in finding the girl I had once been.

Coincidentally, seeking therapy was a requirement for my master's program in counseling. Every good counselor should experience what it's like on the patient's end, but every counselor also needs someone to help them process the cognitive load that they carry.

I was in a session with my new counselor when there was a lengthy pause in the conversation.

The question he had asked me was, "If you could sit across from the old you, what would you want to ask yourself?" I opened my mouth to speak and realized that I had nothing to say! I came up dry.

Finally, I responded, "There's nothing I want to hear from *that* me."

He asked, "Then why do you want to get back to being *that* you?"

And that was the moment that it hit me. I took a deep breath and said, "*That* version of me doesn't exist anymore. I couldn't be *that* me in *this* life. It wouldn't work."

While I look back fondly upon my vivacious, adventurous, and strong-spirited former self, since then I've become something different and something *more*.

His last question that day was, "So, what do you do now?"

Now? Now I need to figure out who I *want* to be. Above all else, I want to become the best version of myself possible. For my son and for my husband (who hasn't given up on me in all my manic soul searching), but really, this is for me. Because my dreams, hopes, and feelings matter.

I matter.

## 4:45AM CONVOS WITH CAM

### MARCH 19, 2014

This morning, my darling son woke up at 4:45 and ran to the big window at the front of our bedroom. He ducked under the giant shade and exclaimed, "Wook! Da moon!"

We had been looking each evening to see the growing moon, but it's been overcast. I ducked underneath the shade with him.

"Yeah, buddy, that's the moon! Isn't it beautiful?"

"Da Tars!"

"Yeah, those stars are *really* bright over the city! Wow!"

"Da pwanet."

"No, baby, those are stars."

I went to grab the iPad in order to pull up the Star Chart app and check myself. As I was doing this, the thought crossed my mind that this is the same kid who can identify any of the planets.

And then I pointed the iPad at the section of sky to reveal...

Yep. That's Mars.

— · —

# TEAM CAM

## NOVEMBER 12, 2014

E xactly two years ago, our family's world was shaken by a word that
describes a developmental disorder that appears in the first three
years of life and impacts the brain's normal development of social and
communication skills.

*Autism.*

For any parent, this word is heavy enough to nearly drown you. Just before
his second birthday, Cam abruptly stopped communicating, no longer
made eye contact, and retreated into himself, creating a divide the size of
the Grand Canyon between us. I can tell you firsthand that this was the
greatest heartbreak I have ever known. When the changes happened, it was
so quick, so we sought the best medical professionals in the field and came
home with a diagnosis that changed everything we knew about our world.

We made the painful decision to sell our home, leave our community, the
jobs that we loved, and our friends and family in Austin, TX, to pursue the
best intensive early intervention that was available. We knew Cam was at
a critical point in his development, which made this choice relatively easy.
That doesn't mean our hearts didn't break when we left.

New York, possessing the reputation of having the best intensive early
intervention services, offered us the promise of a brighter future for our
son. This promise came to fruition via an amazing full-day preschool
designed for children with autism, providing a plethora of special
education services, including occupational, physical, and speech therapies,
as well as transportation to and from school. Cam loved getting on his

school bus each morning and going to school. We all fell deeply in love with his teachers, who are some of the hardest-working professional educators and therapists I have ever had the pleasure of knowing.

Cam's preschool, QSAC (Quality Services for the Autism Community), came through on the promise. When Cam arrived in New York, he was three years old and making one-word utterances in order to meet his basic demands. "Milk." "Snack." "Up."

A year and a half later, Cam is speaking in sentences, including attributes, adjectives, and pronouns.

At the beginning of this adventure, my goal for my son was pretty basic. I wanted him to be just like every other child. I didn't want anyone to know or guess that anything was wrong with him. Today, after experiencing my own ridiculous amount of growth on our adventure, I know that there's absolutely *nothing* wrong with Cam. If you know him, you already know that he couldn't possibly be *just like every other child* because he's Cam!

Allow me to explain.

The other morning, as he played his toy piano, he sang "Twinkle, Twinkle, Little Star." He stopped mid-verse and switched to "Baa Baa Black Sheep." He giggled to himself and started singing his "ABCs."

OK, I realize that I'm a full-grown, educated adult and all, but it honestly never occurred to me that these three songs have the same melody. Cam figured it out, like he does. He's four years old. He also knows more about the solar system than most 12-year-olds, and figured out how to count by twos without instruction. This kid can learn and master most material faster than his teachers can teach it, and he can figure out how things work faster than you can try to keep those things out of reach. Perhaps my favorite thing about him is how much he cares for those around him. He has a loving and goofy heart the size of Texas.

Over the past two years, our adventures have led us through the murky seas of intervention, parenting, love, and reflection. Together, we have grown more than I ever imagined possible. Between the early intervention, exposure to the city and the ocean, and the love and support from our New York friends and family, we are in an entirely different place than we were two years ago.

This weekend, we can return to all the things that we left behind in our beautiful community of Austin, where the support that we received when Cam was diagnosed has never faltered. The love that was sent from afar has kept our hearts tied to a place that we didn't believe we could ever return to. Rob and I haven't been able to imagine anywhere we would put down our roots again, and we couldn't quite commit to *here*. We now know that this is probably because those roots that we planted are still growing where we left them. Will this always be the case? We honestly don't know. We'll go wherever these adventures lead us, and Cam's needs will dictate that direction.

Team Cam (*all over the world*) has been the constant light in our darkness, the shoulder we've cried on, the immeasurable support, and the voice that has given us the courage to press on even during the scary parts. We couldn't have done any of this without them.

The past two years have been the most challenging, frightening, beautiful, difficult, awesome, and incredible years of my life. These days, my endgame is simple: to provide my child with all the tools and skills he needs to be the best possible version of himself. I hope to use my voice to help other parents who may have experienced similar challenges. My goal is to help people understand not only what autism is but also what it isn't. I want to build a community of love and support so that my child always understands that he's got a village, and together we have raised him.

I want people to look at my son and truly see him.

I want my son to feel celebrated, supported, loved, and proud of who he is. To look in the mirror and see all the parts that make up who he is. I want him to truly see all the parts of himself and realize that he is magnificent.

Because, if you know Cam, he really is.

## Summertime Slivers

Because I'm all about authenticity and letting y'all see into the reality of our lives, where it's not always easy.

Here's some insight into what happened thirty seconds after posting some precious summer photos to social media...

Cam declared he needed a bandage with hearts on it. I looked at his foot and discovered a giant splinter in it.

*Great.*

Fast forward past a few minutes of us trying to explain to Cam what was about to go down.

Rob and I began wrestling the angry octopus (aka Cam) as we tried to remove it from his foot (unsuccessfully), all the while listening to his blood-curdling screams and random phrases that sort of made sense to us, his torturers.

"Stop it, I'm awake!"

"No, that's not nice!"

"I gotta go potty!" (His go-to phrase for escape!)

"It's time to take a nap!"

I am amazed that the police didn't knock on our door. This is our life, as real as it gets. It's true, hilarious, and a bit heart-wrenching at the same time. No amount of soothing words from his loving parents could calm his fears as soon as he saw those tweezers.

Eventually, we returned to playing outside again with the heart-covered bandage atop the splinter and high hopes of some black drawing salve pulling that bad boy out or one of us creeping into his room like a tweezer ninja as he sleeps tonight.

# I Was Born in a Small Town

## July 16, 2015

*No, I cannot forget from where it is that I come from*
*Cannot forget the people who love me*
*I can be myself here in this small town*
*And people let me be just what I want to be*
~John Mellencamp

S ome of my very first memories of what it meant to live in a small town were of my desperate dreams of escaping it. I remember feeling so caged in that I could barely breathe. It was too small and boring; there wasn't ever anything to do, and nothing exciting ever happened there. Everyone knew everybody else's business, and therefore everyone knew when you got into trouble. Not only that, but they knew what you did, who was involved, and exactly how you got caught. And they knew it by 9 a.m. the next morning.

Our kind of trouble consisted of sneaking out at night to watch meteor showers on a friend's roof, driving around at night before we had our licenses, and spinning out in snowy parking lots for fun. We made our own adventures in our too-small town. As we grew up, our most dangerous tales were of driving down vineyard rows in a Pinto or swiping a road cone from a construction site and then guiltily taking it back.

When things were really slow, we'd meet out in the middle of nowhere to throw a bonfire party where we thought we were totally hidden. As if it wasn't bound to be interrupted by the police, who knew us each by name, or the occasional coach dragging us out of our teenage reverie. It was good, clean fun that never amounted to too much trouble because we all kept each other honest and took great pains to make sure that we all made it home safe.

I realize now that our town and the experiences of growing up in it were more than beautiful—They were magnificent.

When the hills turned into a brilliant autumnal tapestry or the fog crept up lazily off of Seneca Lake each morning it was breathtaking.

The annual pep rally bonfire, the love of a Saturday morning football game and the delight of the occasional night game under the lights of a rival team. Our one-stoplight town didn't have lights at the football field back then, but these days you might find the whole damn town at a game!

Teachers who always had time to listen. And still do.

Our bus drivers proudly honking their horns after every victory, no matter how small.

Finding my uncle and grandfather at the corner restaurant after school whenever I needed some cash.

Walking to and from school at all hours without fear.

Ice skating on the basketball courts outside when they froze over, and sledding down every hill in town. Seriously, if you had a hill you knew your snow was fair game.

Square dancing in PE class, and if I'm being honest, I was a bit traumatized by this.

Wading in the creek (that most people pronounce "crick") and hunting for crawfish (which most of us called crayfish).

The roar of the Friday night races and watching my Uncle Bill (#82) win. A lot.

Learning to drive alongside horse and buggies.

I remember being walked home from school by a friend when kids were being horribly cruel, as they sometimes are.

That same friend tried to hit me and my girlfriends with a BB gun from his bedroom window a few years later. We're still friends.

There are so many memories, and the beauty of each one resonates in the feelings that I have for the people.

Many years have come and gone, but those relationships? They are still so strong, and that's a testament to that small town and how it raised us.

These memories have come bubbling to the surface recently because, contrary to all of my attempts to escape that small town, I am now at a point in my life where I'm desperately trying to recreate it. I've lived and worked in two of the biggest cities in our country, but I'd much rather find myself in a rebuilt Chevy pickup truck hauling flowers back to a tiny house on some land. I want nothing more than for my son to experience the freedom and sense of community that comes with growing up in a small town.

Yes, there were bad times, too, and they tainted my life with a few memories that perhaps, one day, I will put on paper. But through it all, I always knew that I was part of something truly beautiful, and bigger than myself.

But not too big.

# PADDLE OUT

## JULY 20, 2015

L ast year, I decided that waiting for the day when I might face death
was a horrible time to knock items off the good old bucket list. I had
witnessed some of my bravest friends fight great odds against cancer, and
it hit me hard.

I spent many winter mornings watching the surfers of Long Beach don
their thick wet suits, hoodies, and boots, embrace their boards, and head
out into the frigid water. Their synchronous movements mesmerized me,
as did the delicate yet athletic dance they performed with the waves.

Inspired by the beauty and compelling call of the water, I started with
number 1 on the list: *Learn to Surf.* As romantic or cliché as it sounds, I
had waited my whole life for what was now within my reach.

I was equal parts inspired and terrified.

In the last decade, I've developed an irrational fear of sharks. I can work
myself into a tizzy imagining how I might die in a violent shark attack. I'm
sure that there's a total wealth of meaning if we were to psychoanalyze that
one—an insanely violent death in the place where I found the most Zen.

The ocean has always been the place where I am closest to God, to a creator
that is present in every breaking wave and crashing shoreline. I go there to
fill my soul, and I can find my center with ease. I was sure that my love of
the ocean would help me face my fear.

The last thought running through my mind the night before my lesson
was, *Please don't let me get eaten by a shark tomorrow.*

When I woke, a crippling sense of fear spread throughout my body. My mind raced with a dozen different reasons to cancel my lesson. A picture flashed in my mind that a friend had recently posted on social media. It was a wall with the words *Fear is a liar* painted in large, bold letters, and it became my anchor.

I dragged myself out of bed and took a long, hard look at myself in the mirror. My insides were trembling, and a surge of adrenaline spread outward, reaching my fingertips, which then shook uncontrollably.

I looked at myself again and spoke the words, "You. Have. Survived. Worse." I tried to ignore my fear rather than let it take over, as it clearly intended to do, but this would not be how my story played out. Determined not to be the girl who caved in to fear, I went to my lesson. I showed up because that's how we get past the stuff that scares us.

On the sandy shores of Long Beach, I learned the art of popping up onto the board and that I'm clearly a *goofy foot*, placing my right foot at the head of the board with my left at the back. I spent about 15 minutes practicing this until the instructor and I both agreed that it was time to try it in the water. I lifted my board and awkwardly entered the water. When I ventured in deep enough, I pulled my body on top of the board. I realized I couldn't see anything below me in the water because I was looking toward the incoming waves. I listened to the instructor explain how to determine which waves were worthy and which wouldn't carry me at all. I saw his lips moving, and although I understood what he was saying, a voice (*fear*, no doubt) spoke over his instructions.

*You can't see the sharks.*

Again, the surge of adrenaline pushed through my veins like a sick and toxic drug.

I've struggled with anxiety throughout my life, and although I wish there was a great trick I've developed that helps me in times like this, there isn't one. The instructor continued speaking as I gazed at his calm face. He was certain that I was about to catch my first wave, and I was sure I was about to die.

Amidst the pounding of my heartbeat in my ears, I dug as far down as possible to salvage any remnant of courage that I had left. I came up empty and stared at my instructor.

"Paddle out."

I looked up and saw this knowing smile that suddenly held so much more meaning than before as he said, "Go on, paddle out!"

I honestly don't know what happened at that moment. I looked out at the ocean, and as I watched the waves coming toward me, I noticed the arms next to my board pushing through the water so effortlessly, propelling me forward and into the blue.

There was such grace in the arms—a sense of purpose beyond the levels of anxiety my mind was trying to trap me in. I looked at the hands as they cut through the blue and followed them back to the arms.

My arms.

Pushing through the water, breaking the waves, and allowing my board to sail into the cresting waves; my arms led me. I grabbed the sides of my board and pulled it toward my chest as an enormous wave rolled under and then over me. I was under the waves.

I was *in* the wave.

I was free.

I strived to push my face through the surface in what seemed like an eternity but was truly only an instant. Instinctively, I began paddling out again. I looked over my shoulder at my new surfer friend, who had somehow cracked his face into an even bigger grin. He motioned for me to turn my board toward the beach, so I did, and I realized that this was it. I was going to ride this incoming wave into the shore on my surfboard or my ass.

I don't know what it was about the ocean that day.

There are moments in life that don't have explanations; they simply fall into the beautiful simplicity of just being.

The act of paddling out had given me breath and a rhythm that was not my own but belonged to the sea.

As the wave approached, I watched it over my shoulder until I had to paddle furiously toward the shore to catch it. I grasped the board and pulled my legs up under me in a swift, albeit awkward, first pop-up.

I was standing.

I was moving toward the beach.

It took a moment before I realized *I was surfing!*

The proud whooping noises made by the surf instructors carried across the water. When I finally fell from my board, I turned around, somewhat embarrassed by the attention. About ten instructors were waving their hands in the air and clapping over their heads. I had gotten up onto the board on the first try. I must have looked like a brick heading into that shore, but their love for the sport and the thrill of it all spread throughout my body, taking the place of the fear.

The only thing left to do was turn around and paddle out again.

— • —

# BAMs

In a moment of extreme vulnerability, I posted the following on a local forum for parents and caregivers of children with disabilities:

*Hi friends.*

*This is a call for the parents of children on the spectrum. I have a blog that I write as a therapeutic outlet. In it, I hope to discuss the many things that we, as parents, wish people knew about autism. I would also very much like to include guest writers who have autism. I want the full gamut of our experience to be represented because it's so important to be realistic if we truly want to spread awareness and increase understanding and compassion. I'm hoping to use it as a way to educate people about the realities while inserting teachable moments, both happy and hard, that could enlighten others and be passed on in as many settings as possible. I would love any input from anyone who has something to share. What do you wish people knew about autism?*

Because of this post, I collected so many perspectives from amazing parents. The greatest gift, however, was when one mother, Jill, responded in the comments with, *"I'm stalking y'all and noticing that we all live in the same area. Is anyone interested in meeting up sometime for dinner? I haven't done any of this group's activities but would love to find some moms like me to have/give support, specifically with kids on the spectrum. And here you are! LOL. Let me know."*

Y'all... I think I've found my people! Several of us met up at a local restaurant, and the instant connection through sharing our stories was nothing short of amazing! We dubbed ourselves the BAMs, *aka Bad Ass Mamas*. I can't stop smiling.

# THIS PARENT'S GUIDE TO AUTISM

## AUGUST 11, 2015

I wish more people truly understood autism. This thought crosses my mind so often. I have seen parents, teachers, coaches, professionals, and students all make assumptions based on a person's diagnosis before ever getting to know the individual. Ignorance can cause great harm, and I've witnessed it firsthand.

People are quick to jump to, "Have you heard of Temple Grandin?" as the conversation becomes uncomfortable the minute that they learn my child has autism.

Of course I have! She's one of the most prolific autistic voices of our time, and she continues to add so much value to the understanding of *some* of the autistic experiences.

However, Dr. Grandin is not the only person with autism who has become successful.

Measuring success by only including those who appear to be very *high functioning* (this is a term that we need to move away from, by the way) would be completely missing the mark. Most parents of teenage girls think that their own daughters are very successful, yet they wouldn't compare them to Malala Yousafzai.

I believe people mean well, but sometimes their flippant comments are more heartbreaking than anything else we have gone through as a family.

Allow me to present a few examples that we repeatedly encounter. Some of these are from a collaboration with a few amazing mamas I share a particular bond with!

10. *"Oh, we know someone with autism."*

You know that if you've met one person with autism, you've met *one* person with autism, right?

9. *"I'm so sorry."*

For what? There's no need for an apology.

8. *"He doesn't look autistic!"*

Banging my head on the wall inside my mind.

7. *"Are you sure? He might outgrow it."*

That's not really how it works. And yes, we're sure. The neurologist, developmental pediatrician, behavior analyst, and therapist that we work with are all in agreement. Autism is part of who he is, forever.

6. *"Will you have another child?"*

I really struggle with this one. I'm not sure why anyone thinks this is their business, and part of me wonders if they think our first child was a mistake.

5. *"Do you think vaccinations caused it?"*

Listen. When you ask me this question, not only are you assuming that a choice that I made for my child's health *hurt* him, but you are also ignoring a plethora of evidence to the contrary. C'mon.

(5 is always followed by)

4. *"What do you think caused it?"*

Autism is a spectrum of very complex neurodevelopmental disorders. There are many components involved, including genetics.

(Immediately followed by)

3. *"Oh. Do you think it was you or your husband that passed it down?"*

You realize there is a difference between heredity and genetics, right?

2. *"Does he have any special skills or super powers, <insert uncomfortable laugh>?"*

Indeed, he is a badass. What about your kid?

(And my favorite)

1. *"Oh, he's going to be just fine!"*

He's already fine. In fact, he's amazing. He is the most amazing kid I've ever encountered, but not just because he's mine. See my answer for #2.

I wish you knew more about life alongside autism. I believe that the power lies in educating everyone that we encounter, and the only way to do that is by explaining our experience. However, you'll only see a slice of our reality, as I already mentioned. We are only one set of many parents who share a similarity, but I promise you that the experience of autism is so complicated that you can't stamp us all out into perfect little cookie cutter shapes.

The hard truth to explain is that I only see a tiny speck of what it's like. I'm not autistic. I'm just one fierce warrior mama, and until my son can explain his experience succinctly to me, I'll do my best to translate from my point of view.

There are many, many lists of all the things that you should never say, do, or tell a parent of a child with autism or any disability. Those lists are probably exactly like the one above. Please don't worry about committing them to memory so that you can avoid them.

What I really wish you would commit to is learning more about autism. And please don't lean on me as your sole teacher because, on some days, I'm barely treading water. Learn about autism and then teach your children too. Learn from real people who live with autism every single

day. Start by learning from autistic people. They have important things to s
hare.

*Join me* in learning about the autism experience. I hope we can all learn
from each other.

The statistics are astounding. In fact, the prevalence is on the rise, so the
chances that you will know, love, and work with someone with autism are
growing. Knowledge is power, people. Get to it.

PS: Please stop saying the R word. It's never appropriate.

— · —

# THOUGHTS FOR MY YOUNGER SELF

## DECEMBER 24, 2015

They say that with age comes wisdom, but I don't entirely agree. In my experience, with age comes life experience, and with those experiences, we are open to a whole series of opportunities to learn. Of all the lessons in life, these are the ones I wish I had mastered much earlier.

*Kindness:* This is the number one tool to use. It takes so little energy to give, and the rewards are so impactful.

*Self-confidence:* not to be confused with arrogance, attention-seeking, or self-righteousness. But the knowledge that I am a work in progress and that I'm proud of the progress I'm making. Be proud of all that you've accomplished, despite great odds.

*Self-respect and, with that, boundaries:* the message that you put out into the universe about who you are, how you act, and the caliber of people you want in your life—it all creates the formula for a life that will become your reality. You set the tone for how others perceive, treat, and remember you.

*Stoke the fire:* Follow that inner voice that says, "This world is broken, and we need to fix it!" You are not an idealist; you have ideas. Some of them will work, some of them will fail, and some of these failures will break your heart greatly. Ignore the voices that tell you that you can't fix everything, because that fire inside is exactly what it is for. It's the fuel for the overwhelming passion that has led you through this life. It will not consume you if you put it to good use. Well, it might. Either way, rage on. But remember to rest too.

*Love:* freely giving love to everyone because everyone is deserving, as opposed to only giving what we feel people deserve when they are in our good graces.

*Knowledge:* this does not come as a guaranteed partner for our aging minds and bodies. You have to do the work in this life in order to learn as much as you can about it. Sometimes, what we learn is what we expected. Other times, we dust ourselves off from a battle of wits with life's lessons. We only learn from the lessons that we open ourselves up to. If we reject all that isn't aligned with our current beliefs and systems of understanding, we miss out on so much. Find teachers you respect and learn from them. These people will be knee deep in the most important work of their/your life. Study them. Read their research. Explore their ideas, question everything, and then add what you need to your toolbox. Grow from it. Then, go find more teachers. Never stop learning. A

*Compassion:* when we're angry, joyful, resentful, or afraid, and when we are at our worst, not only when we are at our best. Have compassion for others and for yourself.

*Find your people:* they may not be who you think. They may even find you first. But these are the people who will have your back when you need it, and they will tell you when you've screwed up, too. They will also be the people that you can simply be present with, without frills, pretenses, makeup, or even a shower. They will love you with a passion that fills your heart with abounding joy. They may or may not be family, and they may be constantly growing themselves. Support their journey as fiercely as they are supporting yours.

You've got this.

# To the Little Girl at Recess

### April 6, 2016

To the little girl who held my son's hand today during kindergarten recess... You don't know me, but I'm Cam's mama.

I have been waiting and wishing for someone like you to come along for a very long time. You see, Cam is different in a wonderful sort of way.

He has autism.

That means that there are certain things that might come easily for you that Cam struggles with *greatly*. Things like talking and making friends are enormous challenges that we have been working on for years. I used to wonder if Cam would ever have special friends in his life that he could turn to when he needed them. As his mama, I try to listen, play, and just be there for him.

But I also know the value of a good friend.

It hurts my heart to think that he might not connect with people in that way. Not like he does with his mama. Even though, in some ways, he is just like other children, I wonder if Cam is starting to notice that he's different.

He is *so* smart, and he notices the tiniest details in the most wonderful things.

He learns some things quickly, like the names of all the planets in our solar system and many of their moons!

He's also great at reading sight words!

Some things take a lot of practice, like making those same words come through the difficult journey, starting in his brain and ending in our ears.

Words are not his native language.

Pictures likely are, and he remembers *everything*.

So, I wonder if he sees the incredible beauty in the differences and in himself.

I hope he does.

Today, *you did*. You saw through the differences and right to his heart. You made a friend on the playground and held his hand as the two of you walked, talked, and played together in the sunshine. He enjoyed your friendship so much that he sought you out later in gym class.

I'm pretty sure that his teacher cried.

Gosh, I sure did.

I hope that someone took the time to explain how precious it was that Cam was searching for words to talk to you. Because for him, that is *a lot* of work, but he clearly thought that it was worth it.

I wish I knew your name so that I could thank you and foster your new friendship. I wish I could hug your mama or daddy because they've given you an incredible gift that you shared with Cam today: *the ability to truly see him and reach out to him in the purest form of friendship.*

Autism awareness?

Autism Acceptance.

*Edit: Today, at pick-up, your name was the first thing he mentioned when I asked about his day... Rayanna.*

—  •  —

## The Student Becomes the Master

### May 11, 2016

C onfession: I'm human. I have moments when things are simply too heavy or too much to handle, and it's during times like these that I slink away to cry in private. Few things are as cathartic for me as a good ol' cry. Probably because I hold so much in. Today, for many compounded and complicated reasons, as I sat down in my car, I burst into tears in front of Cam, which *never* happens. I try not to become overly emotional in front of him because he is easily overwhelmed, and sometimes what he doesn't understand frightens him.

As I quickly tried to regain my composure, I heard his little voice from the backseat.

Slowly and quietly, he said, "Take a deep breath. Mama, wipe your tears. Take a deep breath. Calm down."

And then he modeled deep breaths until I joined him. Just like I have done for him so many times before.

As difficult as some days can be, I am so grateful to be his mama. As fearful as I am when things are going wrong, I am so often reminded that we are doing this parenting thing right.

Thanks, Cam.

Let's try again tomorrow.

# Today, Gladiator!

November 8, 2016

T he thing that I rarely speak of as a parent of a child with special needs is the never-ending fight to make sure that your child is being cared for, educated, and treated in such a way that will allow him or her to fulfill their ultimate potential. The level of vigilance that is required to ensure all members of the team are consistently acting in the best interest of your child is both overwhelming and unsustainable.

It's imperative, but my God, it's exhausting.

Not to mention managing the team. Coordinating multiple providers of therapy several days a week, both private and within schools, the team of educators, after-school care providers, coaches, and family. Our diligence is often emphasized by the pangs of guilt we feel as we turn down rare playdate invites or extra-curricular activities like sports or boy scouts because our therapy schedule often won't allow it. We stay the course, fully aware that the therapy is providing more progress than we've ever seen before.

We push on, knowing that we are fighting for what is right for our child at this moment.

Friends who work in education, please keep this in mind when you see us in an IEP meeting and we're depleted, defensive, and emotional. While you may plan for the school year, we're planning for a lifetime. That meeting simply represents another step, and we aren't yet sure if it is going to result in creating a team of champions or require us to gear up for the role of gladiator, yet again, in another fight for what our child needs.

*The credit belongs to the man who is actually in the arena, whose face is marred by dust and sweat and blood; who strives valiantly; who errs, who comes short again and again, because there is no effort without error and shortcoming; but who does actually strive to do the deeds; who knows great enthusiasms, the great devotions; who spends himself in a worthy cause; who at the best knows in the end the triumph of high achievement, and who at the worst, if he fails, at least fails while daring greatly.*

-Theodore Roosevelt

— · —

# MAMASTAY

## DECEMBER 12, 2018

C am and I began an adventure in mindfulness when he was between three and four years old. Truly, it was out of a sense of self-preservation and desperation. During a meltdown, I needed to give him some space and also give myself about ten deep breaths to find my calm in order to tend to his needs. A meltdown for a child with autism is *nothing* like a tantrum. It's a symptom of intense distress when the delicate sensory balance has tipped and their emotional regulation spirals completely out of their control. Cam's last meltdown was four years ago. I'm not saying he'll never have another one, but we both have the tools now if he does.

He knows how to find his own sense of calm because I taught him the foundations when he was already there, so that when he felt himself spiral, he could access his tools. You can't learn how to access your tools when you're in a heightened state of emotional dysregulation. If we're being honest, I know plenty of neurotypical adults who struggle with this concept. Teaching this skill to Cam took practice and creating a habit of intentionally pausing in the moment to acknowledge our bodily sensations and what the precise emotion was that he might be feeling. Looking back, I learned so much about mindfulness through these moments.

To this day, Cam still says "Mamastay." It's one of the *Camisms* I will never correct because I know I will mourn when he self-corrects it one day and it's gone.

## Sacred Firsts

### December 16, 2018

C am was super silent yesterday morning, and when Rob went to check on him, he was lying on the floor of his playroom coloring. This had *never* happened before.

Hoping we could get him to color again, we set up an art station for him this morning with easy access to coloring books, crayons, markers, and colored pencils. Cam has always struggled to hold his attention long enough to enjoy coloring. It's been a fight to explain staying within the lines or producing quality work because he has always rushed through it just to get it done. Eventually, we let it go because, in the grand scheme of things, it's not a priority.

He was upstairs playing while I was downstairs cleaning. He hollered down, "Mama! I am coloring so nicely!" I immediately went upstairs to find him sitting at his little station and happily coloring. I praised him and his work and came back downstairs, where I sat for a few minutes, crying silent, joyful tears.

A few moments later, he yelled down again, "Mama, can you color with me?"

I pulled my shit together real quick so that I could color with my son for the first time without a fight and, this time, with an official invitation.

Sometimes the simplest things are the most beautiful.

— ◦ —

# Valentime's

### February 14, 2019

As an adult, I've never really bought into Valentine's Day. I can appreciate its meaning for those who celebrate it. I simply haven't ever gotten all wrapped up in it.

Until now.

Last night, Cam sat at the table with me, excitedly filling out 25+ cards for his classmates and teachers. He took great pains to make sure that each one was his best writing, insisting that he start over with any that got smudged.

I used to have to reinforce each card with mini-chocolate chips because his fine motor skills made writing really difficult for him, and he just didn't have any interest in participating. It felt like work to him back then. By card number 3, he would insist I increase the chips exponentially. That's *a lot* of chocolate chips.

He woke up this morning and excitedly proclaimed, "It's Valentime's, Mama!" And then his face erupted into the biggest smile. My child, who struggles immensely with social interaction and communication, cannot wait to give his cards to his classmates.

That, apparently, is what it's all about.

# CONFESSIONS AT THE DOCTOR'S OFFICE

## FEBRUARY 15, 2019

R ecently, with the guidance of Cam's neurologist, Rob and I have been considering starting a prescription stimulant to address Cam's symptoms of ADHD. It's been so difficult to tease apart where autism ends and ADHD begins, but we aren't treating the disability. We were hoping to treat the symptoms that seem to make learning and sustained attention so difficult for Cam. However, until this point, we have used every viable tool to address the symptoms, which are primarily hyperactivity, impulsivity, difficulty focusing, etc.

Of course, before I agree to incorporate anything (therapy or medication), I dive deep down the rabbit hole and read every piece of evidence-based literature that I can get my hands on. Our neurologist was incredibly helpful in determining which vital nutrients Cam might be deficient in, and we started there. In controlled trials, we added NAC (N-Acetylcysteine), omega-3s, magnesium, and a vitamin B complex. All of them seemed to provide minimal improvements, but nothing promised the type of improvement that is noted with the addition of a stimulant. Hesitantly, I agreed to a trial, and I had Cam's prescription filled at our local pharmacy.

I stared at that bottle for two weeks before I had the nerve to open it. At night, I would lie awake worrying that he might not be able to adequately express how it made him feel. What if it scared or startled him? Would he become dysregulated at school? Would he know to tell someone if it felt wrong?

One morning, I opened up the bottle as I was doling out his daily vitamins, and before I gave it much thought, I popped one in my mouth and washed it down with coffee.

You might wonder what would make a grown adult do something so impulsively. The irony of that moment stays with me.

The simplest explanation for my rash behavior was that I decided (in 2.2 seconds) to trial it myself before giving it to him.

Impulsive? You betcha!

I thought little of it until I finished rushing through our early morning routine, dropped the man-cub off at school, and hurried to work. A few hours later, as I was sitting in a meeting, it hit me.

Throughout my entire life, there has been a source of constant chatter in my mind. Remember my noisy initial adventures in mindfulness? Well, on this day, everything changed. As I listened to my colleagues discuss current projects, problems to be addressed, and initiatives that we wanted to roll out, it startled me to realize that my mind had become *quiet*.

During these meetings, I've always felt as if every new topic we discussed opened a new tab in my mind where the good ol' brain trust began hyper-focusing. Immediately, I am thrust into problem-solving mode, only to be interrupted by the next topic and a new tab opening, repeating until the meeting is over and I feel completely exhausted.

I sat quietly in the meeting, in awe of the newfound silence in my head. My boss noticed the change in my behavior, and after the meeting, he asked me if everything was alright.

I laughed and said, "Yeah. Everything is great, actually. I'm just in shock!"

Confused, he asked, "Shocked about which part?"

"I guess I'm shocked that all of y'all have this kind of quiet happening in your heads all the time!"

And then I confessed that I had taken one of Cam's stimulants to be sure that it wouldn't make him feel out of control.

He laughed and said, "Yeah, there's probably a reason for that."

Rude, right?

As luck would have it, I had a previously scheduled appointment with my neurologist that Friday. I struggle with migraines, and we were evaluating how a new injectable medication might work for me. We planned to begin the medication trial that day, but as soon as she picked up the needle, I interrupted her and burst into another confession.

It has always amazed me that some people can tell a story that starts at point A and ends at point B. I take people on a complete adventure, which is good for storytelling but kind of awkward in the doctor's office.

I wrapped up with, "Listen, I'm a school counselor, and I do not abuse drugs. This is not something that I've ever done before, but I figured I should tell you in case it impacts me trialing this medication."

And then she laughed.

"Well, Danielle, that's because you most certainly have ADHD."

During prior visits, she and I frequently discussed my coping strategies for stress, which included yoga, meditation, walking, etc. She thought I knew I had ADHD, and because I had even brought up my concerns about medicating Cam, she had assumed that I preferred not to medicate myself to treat the symptoms that appeared to be minimally impacting me.

Let me just clarify, for the record, that if you've never had a moment of silence in your entire life, you don't realize what you're missing. A plethora of self-designed coping strategies could not compete with the realization that my world felt different because my brain *was* different.

That day was a complete game-changer for me. I dove into the research that highlighted how ADHD presents in girls and women. I could check every single box on every single list, but it had never occurred to me because I thought I was functioning just fine. Learning about and understanding how ADHD impacted my life was the best tool that I've ever added to my toolbox. I learned to recognize my own needs and patterns of behavior that I had tried to suppress for so many years. For example, I can "people" all day, but when that day is over, I have exceeded my bandwidth and want to crawl under Cam's weighted blanket and hide. Unfortunately, I do not have the essential gauge that most people possess that signals, *Hey, you've interacted, eaten, drank, or exerted yourself too much!* Nope, I plow through life like a bull in a china shop, accomplishing all of my goals and responsibilities until I'm completely depleted and inevitably crash.

So, it was with a brand new ADHD diagnosis at 44 years old that I started to truly understand myself, my needs, and how much I could relate to Cam. Many aspects of life had always been an enigma to me because they seemed so much easier for everyone else while I hid my struggle. I finally realized why, and it may have been the most liberating moment in my adult life so far.

One truth that I've learned about neurodivergent brains is that we are so used to working at a capacity that is beyond typical bandwidth (filtering our environment, constant sensory overwhelm, mental chatter, etc.) that we don't recognize when we have completely exceeded our own.

Chaos is often our baseline; the magic is in understanding *why*.

# SORRY, ROB

## FEBRUARY 21, 2019

Today, when I picked Cam up from his after-school program, the teacher of his group politely reminded me that after-school snacks are supposed to be healthy, but that today Cam pulled out a bag of Fruit Loops and a bag of Doritos.

I was mortified.

Rob packs Cam's lunch in the morning, and *he knows* the rules for both school and after-school snacks! I didn't even know we had Fruit Loops! I apologized and promised that it wouldn't happen again.

I took Cam home and proceeded to angry clean until Rob walked in the door. I was vacuuming and turned off the machine just in time to climb upon my soapbox and explain that Cam got into trouble for bringing Fruit Loops and Doritos for snacks.

*Rob laughed.*

I tried not to make a big deal out of it at first, but I've been warning him since kindergarten! We all know teachers can be judgy about everyone else's parenting skills, and the last thing I needed was for Cam's teachers to think we didn't care about his diet.

It's not funny when I'm the one who has to explain that my kid's favorite food group is crunchy orange carbs. Yes, there's the occasional carrot, but this kid loves any cracker-based snack covered in cheddar.

I *swear* we feed him healthy food.

When Rob stopped laughing, he said, "I didn't pack Fruit Loops *or* Doritos."

Stunned, I went into our bedroom where Cam was enjoying his afternoon iPad time.

"Cam, where did you get the Fruit Loops and the Doritos that you had today?"

"At school."

I was so confused. I stood there staring at him for several seconds. He looked up from his iPad and coolly said, "I got it at lunch."

Now it was me who laughed! "Cam, did you buy them at the snack counter at lunch?" He gets an allowance in his lunch account every Friday for ice cream!

"Yes."

I couldn't believe it. "Why did you buy them?"

"To have a snack after school." And then he looked at me like I was crazy.

My dear friend Alison pointed out that he's clearly making progress with his executive functioning skills:

- planning ahead

- making a purchase

- saving for later

Sorry, Rob.

# STARRY, STARRY NIGHT

## MAY 5, 2019

C am has a love for creating art that he's not been able to fully express until recently.

Yesterday, I took a nap. This is a *huge* rarity in our world because I barely stop moving during the waking hours.

When I came out to the living room, Rob and Cam were at the dining table painting. Without looking up, Cam said, "Good morning, Danielle! Did you sleep well? I'm painting like Vincent Van Gogh."

And he certainly was!

Earlier that day, Cam had asked Rob, "Can I paint like Vincent Van Gogh?" So Rob helped him figure out what painting he was remembering. It turns out that he recalled it from the Baby Einstein DVDs he had when he was 3! This kid's memory is incredible. After they identified which painting Cam was referring to, Rob helped him choose the colors. He gave him a brief lesson, and voila! He patiently worked to recreate Starry Night with his dad's help.

This is something we need to nurture more regularly.

—  •  —

# No Fear

### June 17, 2019

I remember how overwhelmed Cam was the very first time we took him to the beach on Long Island. He was three years old, and he cried in the chaos.

This broke my heart, because the ocean is where I find the most joy, stillness, and healing.

Sensory-wise, it was a nightmare for him. Too loud, too bright, too many people, too many "nos" from us.

For weeks, we would take him to the beach, coax him under the boardwalk, play "baby shark" (before it was a song), and tempt him with Goldfish. He would laugh and squeal (he didn't have many words) and we would reward his every step toward the crashing waves. Some days we would make it another 50 feet toward the water. Some days we'd have to go back ten. By the end of the summer we could all sit together on a blanket by the shore, and eventually Cam would run into the crashing waves with his little feet, and squeal and laugh as he retreated back to the safety of our blanket.

This year, he jumped right out of his comfort zone and surfed with an amazing organization called A Walk on Water.

Today, he wants his own surfboard, and we have to negotiate to get him out of the water.

This is our life, and I love every moment of it.

---•---

# ADVENTURES IN CAMELOT

## JUNE 18, 2019

As we were exploring Galveston yesterday, my phone battery ran out. I was using my phone for navigation, so Rob substituted his for mine, and I was amazed at how much more difficult it was to see his screen! My eyes have taken a downward spiral since I turned 40, going from 20/20 vision to blurry/super light-sensitive. It's mildly annoying and I suppose I should be grateful for a lifetime of healthy eyes. Of course, I immediately start pondering all the many problems that could cause my vision to change so rapidly.

Rob, reassuring as always, said, "It's just your eyes getting older..."

Excuse me? Not today, mister. "They aren't *old* eyes. They are fine!"

I immediately turned to Cam, in the backseat, for backup.

Life lessons learned in #Camelot...

*Never* ask Cam a question that you don't want him to answer honestly.

Me: Cam, is Mama old or young?

Cam: Mama is old.

(Rob and I laughed...)

Rob: You really shouldn't look to him for a pep talk, right now, you know!

Me: (laughing) Hmmm... Is Mama sweet or mean?

Cam: Mama is sweet!

Me: (Thinking: YES! +1 for Mama's hurt feelings!)

Me: Cam, is Mama pretty or ugly?

Cam: Mama is pretty!

Me: (to Rob) HA! That's my boy.

Cam: But... You're not *that* pretty.

Now, there's a line that mustn't ever be crossed in the world of autism and the reinforcement of behavior. Actually, this is true for all behavior, but we find it to be a matter of profound importance in our world.

Laughter, for example, can (accidentally) be a powerful reinforcer for a behavior that we don't want to occur ever again. It's something that both Rob and I work tirelessly to keep in check. Sometimes, when Cam comes out with a new *Camism* we nearly bite off our tongues withholding our laughter.

Much like the time he asked for a third popsicle, when he was 4. He had very limited language and asked, "More?"

When we said "No, you've already had two," he replied with a very exasperated, "That's bullshit..."

Everyone in the room struggled to contain their laughter, turning their backs and walking away until they were safely out of his periphery. Mission accomplished, phew! Even though I wanted to give him that third popsicle for correctly using the new phrase in context, I had to neutralize the power of the phrase that he most likely learned from his Mama.

Yesterday was a different story. Trapped in the front seat of the car, with nowhere to retreat to in order to hide our laughter, Rob and I burst into the most raucous cacophony of laughter you could imagine. I had tears rolling down my face. Rob was cackling so hard he looked like he needed oxygen. Cam was absolutely delighted by his own humor. We still have no idea where he learned this phrase, or if it's just one of the many things that he's thinking that he lets out when he's finally comfortable with the pattern of words he's strung together...

Social skills training in the moment: When we caught our breath, we explained that while sometimes we want to tell people exactly what we are thinking, we have to hold our thoughts back to avoid hurting someone's feelings. In essence, not everything that crosses our minds needs to come out of our mouths. We promised him he can always tell *us* exactly what he's thinking, and we will help him learn if it's something that should be said out loud or simply thought.

From the back seat, as Rob and I continued to bask in the ripples of our stifled laughter, I heard Cam say, "But my Mama *is* pretty."

— · —

# Movie Talk

## July 7, 2019

C am finds great comfort in scripting lines from his favorite movies. I've noticed how frequently he asks to have *movie talk* when he wants to be involved in the interaction or conversation but isn't sure how to interject.

I get it! It's *so* much more comfortable when you know what to expect in the conversation. When language and social skills are your greatest challenges and anticipation is your kryptonite, taking the risk of interjecting must be terrifying! Scripting is comforting and makes him feel less isolated. I wonder how often teachers or peers misinterpret his behaviors, leaving them to think that his silence means he *wants* to be isolated.

Social anxiety is an enigma for those who develop social skills easily, and that breaks my heart.

What may appear to be nonfunctional behavior is a valid part of his language development. I remember various professionals encouraging us to ignore the scripts to force him to engage in *functional communication*. I'm grateful that we went with our gut, and didn't listen to them.

Cam, like many people on the autism spectrum, is a gestalt language processor, learning and developing language skills in entire strands of language rather than building single words into phrases. He pulls the strands in, analyzes them, uses them in scripts, and then eventually he pulls the strand apart and the words are all accessible to him in many combinations. If you're not familiar with GLP, I highly recommend taking a peek at any of the beautifully illustrated designs online that capture this concept nicely.

These scripted lines provide Cam with the means to take part in back-and-forth conversation, not only with ease, but with confidence. Eventually, he will use pieces of the scripts in context, appropriately, and then he will add them to his repertoire of words. He generalizes this across settings, and it works! That's our Cam, working so hard to open doors to what was once an obstacle to communication. Practice makes it possible.

Recently, I attempted to combine reading practice with his love for a scene between the two main characters in his favorite animated movie. I printed out the script of the scene so that we could read through it together, but of course Cam had memorized nearly every word.

It's worth mentioning that he spent most of the time correcting my messed-up lines with a big goofy grin and lots of giggles. Pure joy radiated off this kid the entire time we exchanged lines.

I'm pretty sure we have a theater kid on our hands, and I am here for it!

—•—

## LAKESIDE CONVERSATIONS WITH CAM

### JULY 11, 2019

I've often wondered if we would ever have truly meaningful conversations that didn't merely address Cam's immediate needs. When your child has limited ways to express themselves, it can be a struggle to learn how to communicate and connect.

Cam is becoming increasingly adept at communicating his thoughts, ideas, and dreams! This morning, he started a conversation about how his dreams fade away when he wakes up.

"And then, (he waves his hand in front of his face and makes a sound like the wind) *schwooooooo!* My dreams are gone."

That he wanted to share this with me was nothing short of soul-filling!

A few things I've learned:

*Every* conversation is truly meaningful.

*Every* connection bridges the gap between our experiences, and there's no way to lessen the magnitude of these moments.

— · —

# Mind Your Manners

## August 3, 2019

P eople often ask me why I share stories about Cam's autism when he's making so much progress.

Some people (erroneously) assume that the progress Cam is making with language and social skills will one day make him *"indistinguishable from his peers."* If you know Cam, you know that there's so much that sets him apart from others. Autism is one component of what makes this kid unique and amazing.

During our summer vacation, I made it a point to teach social skills amid everything we did so that practicing them became an authentic experience, allowing him a greater chance at generalizing the skills:

*When an elevator, subway, or train door opens, we wait for others to step out before trying to step in.*

*Stay in your bubble; don't get too close to people's personal space; it can make others uncomfortable.*

*Say "please" and "thank you" when you are ordering your lunch.*

*Take care of your own garbage and clean up after yourself.*

Y'all, I can tell you that on vacation, one thing that placed this kid well above and beyond his peers (*and* their adults) was that he put a hell of a lot more effort into practicing social skills and manners than *most* people we encountered.

Others (with the best of intentions, I'm sure) often ask if I'm worried that sharing our story will affect how people perceive him one day, knowing that he is autistic. Will it ruin his social life? His love life?

I share our story because I am *not ashamed* of Cam's autism, and I never want him to be. I mostly share our triumphs—most of the hard parts, the ugly experiences, and the heartaches have yet to be shared. There are plenty of them, and if you know those details, you know I struggle to teach all the things to all the people at all times.

I, too, have ugly cried on an airplane, in my car, in the Target dressing room, at IEP meetings—you name it. I've mama-bear-stared at plenty of ignorant passersby who have judged me or Cam for what they did not know or understand. I'm not sure I have the eloquence yet to share the ugly parts without dropping some F-bombs and calling people out for their behavior.

I believe that by highlighting the good; I am purposefully refusing to shine a light on the bad. The love and support we receive from those who follow our adventures shows me that this is working. Plus, many of these stories are not mine to share, they are Cam's. Spotlighting his most difficult moments suggests that his voice and his dignity don't matter. For almost every situation or photo that I've shared, he's given permission to share them. Since he could first communicate, his voice has mattered.

So why do I share so much?

I'm trying to inspire, encourage, and teach people about this journey. I believe it was Maya Angelou who said, "Do the best you can until you know better. Then, when you know better, do better."

Luckily, there's a lot more acceptance happening in our world every day because of a better understanding of autism and more access to knowledge than ever before. I'm not nearly done advocating for my son to be seen, valued, and heard for exactly who he is.

Please continue to teach your children to be kind, accepting, and curious. Please continue to click on the links that I share, read the words, and learn all the things because we need you.

# DESPERATE CRIES

## AUGUST 10, 2019

L ast night, as I was tucking him in, Cam asked me, "Why do songs hurt inside? Right there!" And then he pointed to his chest.

I told him that sometimes music can touch our emotions, and we feel it deeply. Then I asked him what song he was talking about. With a very serious expression, he said that the Peanuts gang sang it, and "they are holding hands, and it is the night." He then told me, dramatically, "It gives m e *desperate cries*, mama! Like the opera!"

A few days ago, inspired by a scene in *Curious George*, Cam began asking questions about opera. So Rob showed him a video of Andrea Bocelli singing "Nessun Dorma." It was beyond beautiful. Cam watched it intently from his "hiding place" on the stairs, staring through the railings, until his eyes welled up with tears and he asked Rob to turn it off.

Honestly, I have the same reaction. Two years ago, I ugly cried through a musical number featuring some of my students singing a song from Dear Evan Hansen.

Just now, after he led me on a wild goose chase on YouTube, I discovered the song he was talking about, the one that he is connecting with on such a deep level that it gives him "desperate cries."

I hovered over "Just One Person" from *Snoopy! The Musical.*

"Yes!" He excitedly proclaimed, "That's the one!"

I wasn't familiar with it, but now it's honestly the most beautiful song I've ever heard.

The little things are almost always the most amazing, gigantic, splendid, soul-filling, and magnificent things.

And he's right. It hurts *right there*.

*If just one person believes in you*
*Deep enough, and strong enough, believes in you*
*Hard enough, and long enough before you knew it*
*Someone else would think, if he can do it, I can do it.*
*Making it... Two!*

Go ahead. Look it up. You're welcome.

# New School Year Ramblings

## August 18, 2019

A t Cam's open house last week, we tried to go early since crowds can be overwhelming for him. Despite our best efforts, a lot of other families went early as well. Cam's anxiety spiked, his language disappeared, and he retreated into his own world. Eventually, we found ourselves surrounded by the chaos, and we exited as quickly as possible.

I left the boys at home to attend my school's 6th grade open house, feeling nervous about what we just experienced, and I slid down the anxiety rabbit hole myself, getting stuck on all the mama bear worries.

Since Cam's open house, the following has happened:

A friend who is also the parent of one of Cam's classmates texted me to tell me that their child saw Cam's name on a desk in their classroom, and he chose the seat right next to his. We were both so happy about them being together.

This morning, in an email from his teacher, I learned that a little girl in his class who he became good friends with last year told the teacher that she had spent the summer "praying that they would be in the same class again."

In that same email thread, the teacher and I have been problem-solving and sharing ideas that are coming from such a beautiful place. The teacher wanted to learn more, so she shared her thoughts and questions to make sure Cam's needs would be met, much like we've been afraid they might not be.

I'll be over here ugly-crying, y'all.

*This* is inclusion. It's not a place, a time, or a thing to be done out of charity. It's the intentional creation of a place where everyone feels a sense of belonging. Where each person feels seen, heard, and valued.

I have fought like a gladiator for years to ensure it was happening with fidelity!

Thanks to #TeamCam, it really is.

Changing mindsets and systems is sometimes uncomfortable. It is a process, and when it's done right, it is life-changing for everyone involved.

— • —

# THE SCIENTIST

## OCTOBER 10, 2019

Last night, Cam had a difficult time falling asleep. As I was lying beside him, trying to determine what his worries were about, he started sobbing. Crying isn't really in his repertoire, so I immediately launched into crisis management mode by wrapping my arms around him and squeezing him tightly, until eventually his breathing matched my own.

When his heavy cry subsided, he said, "Mama, I'm worried about school. I don't want to make bad choices."

This one stung and gave me pause for reflection. Good vs. bad—is there anything in life that is this black and white? I realized our mistake and wondered how we could fix it, but also how we might use this as a teachable moment for all of us. We try not to highlight the negative and intentionally focus on positives, so the internalization of "bad choices" is because we praise him when he makes good choices—something that is quite difficult for a child who struggles with executive functioning, impulsivity, and communication.

Although he has had a great streak of excellent behavior, I could tell the possibility of a behavioral blip was weighing heavily on his little heart. He's such a hard worker, and he gives 100% every single day. Sometimes he can become consumed with how other people perceive him, especially if he's not behaving as expected.

While the rest of his classmates are focused on multiplication facts, he's also focusing on language (both conversational and vocabulary) that he hasn't yet mastered, social skills, and all the sensory input and distractions within the classroom.

Last night, I praised him for the hard work that he puts into everything he does, and the bravery with which he faces each new situation. He's truly incredible, and I want him to believe it to his core.

This morning, on the way to school, he was talking nonstop in the backseat. We spend our morning drives talking about the ways we can try to make it a great day, but this morning he did *all* the talking, and he had a plan.

"I will stay in my seat. I will listen to my teachers. I will follow directions. I will stay with my group. I will use all of my words. I will be kind to my friends. I will make good choices. I will have a great day today, Mama!"

And then, out of nowhere, he started singing Coldplay's "*The Scientist.*"

*Nobody said it was easy.*

*No one ever said it would be this hard.*

*Oh, take me back to the start...*

And just like that, my mama bear's heart shattered into a million pieces. I had no idea that he knew the words to this song. I've often wondered if he would ever connect deeply to people or music. It turns out he already does—maybe he always has, in his own way.

Sometimes, I forget he is *always* thinking, *always* absorbing, and *always* feeling every damn thing at its utmost intensity.

Thanks for the reminder, Cam.

# An Unexpected Plot Twist...

## December 5, 2019

Disclosing deeply personal information on social media can be really overwhelming, because it inevitably leads to many questions, assumptions, and, let's be honest, a lot of judging. Luckily, I'm in a place in my life where I don't feel the need to justify my decisions as an adult to anyone—especially my parenting decisions. But once I've released our story, people have the potential to break my heart or help heal it.

Recently, we have begun a new journey, one that we didn't quite expect to face. I'm not sharing this information because I need or want your advice. Trust me, the amount of evidence-based peer-reviewed medical journals that I have read in the last 6 years is beyond comprehension, but it's led us to exactly where we should be right now.

I'm sharing our story, hoping all that we've learned and experienced will help someone else avoid the pitfalls and pain of our search for answers.

I'll try to tell the story as best as I can, but it isn't linear, so hang on, folks, and bear with the back and forth. If it's confusing or overwhelming for you, try to imagine what it has been like for us.

This summer, while traveling to NY, Rob and I noticed Cam had developed some OCD-related behaviors, including large motor and vocal tics, almost overnight. His anxiety spiked, and he feared things he was comfortable with just days before. He woke several times in the night sweating and afraid, and on the flight back from NY, I counted 45 tics in three minutes. I turned to Rob, seated on the other side of me, and said, "I know what this is."

Upon landing, I called Cam's pediatrician and told her, "I think Cam has strep. And I really think that he has PANDAS."

She agreed to test him for strep, but reminded me she doesn't treat PANDAS but if he tested positive for strep, she would treat that, and then she told us to come on in.

I know that many of you are about to Google Pandas right now, but please trust that I'll get you there.

The strep swab was negative in the pediatrician's office. I was in complete disbelief because something neurological was going on, and I felt it in my gut. I knew beyond any doubt what it was. We had seen behaviors erupt like this before and then go away. "It's PANDAS," I repeated to his pediatrician. She agreed that there was something profound happening, as she could clearly see these behaviors that were not usual for Cam. She stood up, pursed her lips, and advised us to get into our neurologist's office ASAP.

We followed her advice and made an emergency appointment with Cam's neurology office the next day. When the nurse practitioner sat down with us to go over everything, she asked us to start from the beginning. At this point, I was so exhausted by the anxiety I felt over watching the symptoms take over Cam's body, that I erupted in a retelling of all the things that no doctor had ever taken into consideration before but that I felt compelled to say, *again.*

Cam has struggled with recurrent infections since he was two years old, which was right around the time of his diagnosis of autism. Even though he *really* struggles (both physically and behaviorally) when he has any sort of infection that requires an antibiotic, Rob and I almost look forward to what we refer to as the "antibiotic effect." If you're one of our close friends or family, you've witnessed it as well, and we've all sort of marveled at it but used to consider it an anomaly. When Cam gets really sick, he turns into an absolute mess. It looks like a complete behavioral regression. The challenging behaviors skyrocket, no one sleeps, and we all fall apart.

Until about five days into an antibiotic, when all the symptoms decrease,

*All of them.*

Even some symptoms that we have associated with autism since he received his diagnosis.

Let's talk about that for a minute.

Cameron experienced what the developmental specialists referred to as "regressive autism," because even though he was developing typically until he was two, he experienced an abrupt loss of skills. Words went away, eye contact disappeared, he hated sounds, didn't want to be touched, and was completely disengaged from our little family unit. It's been a long road to get where we are today, but worth every single struggle because his progress has been incredible.

Between ages 2 and 3, we've seen the same behaviors and struggles that we know are part of who Cam is. Unless he becomes really sick, then the symptoms are exaggerated and sometimes unmanageable. When he has a fever, he almost always comes through the other side with new skills. Every time we have brought this up to a medical professional, even questioning the possibility of PANDAS, they have explained it as, "Well, if you don't feel well, you often struggle in all areas. That's all it is."

No. It's not.

When Cam is on a broad-spectrum antibiotic, the challenging behaviors disappear, his communication skills improve immensely, and it's like the clouds parted for a few days. His struggles are so much less apparent. It was a wild idea, but one that Rob and I became used to: His struggles that were associated with autism get better, *and* he comes out of the other side with new skills. Eye contact, language, and the ability to focus improve.

Just like that.

Every time.

Why? How? It never made sense. But we knew it was real, and we accepted it as our truth.

It is important to note that we've *never* tried to cure him of autism; as a matter of fact, we've implemented wording in his IEP (individualized education plan) that states that *no one should ever attempt to make him appear less autistic for the benefit of "fitting in" or camouflaging.* We emphasized that educators and support staff should use a strengths-based approach and that his autism should never be treated as a deficit.

So, how did we make sense of what we were seeing? Well, I dove into research and read everything that I could about autism. Quite by accident, I came across the findings of a venture capitalist who worked with biotechnology startups. John Rodakis also discovered the "antibiotic effect" on his own while administering them to his son, who also experienced an abrupt regression of skills.

Wait? What?

A bit of research revealed even more information, including a research study that was being conducted because there appeared to be a plethora of anecdotal evidence from other parents, both about the worsening of symptoms and those that were eased. My heart raced, and I set out to explore the realities of this research.

Then I connected the dots.

You know what else affects Cam's behavior?

Probiotics. If he's not on a quality probiotic, his behavior changes.

If he's on the *wrong* probiotic, his behavior changes.

I know it sounds crazy. But it's not so crazy in our world, and certainly not now that the gut-brain connection is possibly some of the most innovative research being done with implications in neuroscience and the treatment of many mental health issues.

If you're not familiar yet with the gut-brain link and the implications that it has on legitimately *everything* we know about how *what* we eat affects *how* we feel and behave, then take this moment to open another tab next to the one you opened when you googled PANDAS, and I'll wait...

Welcome back.

So then what?

Well, I kept reading research journals. Our close family and friends were along for the ride, and they began noting articles that came across their radars, too, and sending them to me. It was all coming together, but I still had so many questions, and no one, not our pediatrician or our neurologist, had any answers. So we kept reading, searching, hoping, and praying for answers.

Back to this summer's emergency visit to the neurologist. Once I had explained all the above, she cocked her head and asked me if we would submit to blood work. Of course we did, and then we returned home, waiting for answers while large motor tics ravaged Cam's poor little body. He couldn't stop his arms from flailing and punching at the air uncontrollably as he walked around the room, touching every corner of every object. Touching every light switch and perseverating on worries and topics that made little sense to us from the outside.

We were terrified that we were losing our son. Again.

The work that we put in to bring our child back from the initial regression was long and arduous. After thousands of hours of various therapies, years of consistent, constant analysis, and reinforcement of strategies to build on skills, we felt like we were losing ground and no one had any help to give.

The next morning, his pediatrician called. She said, "The lab results came back, and you were right. It *is* strep. What did the neurologist say?"

I filled her in, hung up the phone, and sobbed.

I knew what we were facing. I had been trying to explain the complexities of Cam for six years, and I cried both out of relief and exasperation. Then the neurologist's office called with the results of the blood work, which showed a strep infection and markers for inflammation.

I was right the whole time.

We started antibiotics, and guess what? Skill surge. Behavior decline.

His rate of language acquisition was insane, and he began communicating at a level we had never witnessed.

Even his classroom teachers were in awe of the progress he made, his social interaction, his ability to focus, and how "the clouds just seemed to part" for him while on antibiotics.

And it did last awhile...

The symptoms returned about 5–10 days after they finished the course of antibiotics. Sometimes with a vengeance.

Eventually, the tics returned as well. The OCD. Even emotional lability that is totally out of character for Cam. So, I'd take him back to urgent care for a throat swab, and sure enough, the infection would still be there.

Another antibiotic, but a different type. We tried again. Same results every time.

Imagine the feeling of collecting data and realizing the significance right before your eyes when it's regarding your own child. We were moving toward something huge, and we knew it!

PANDAS. Not cute or cuddly. If I'm being honest, it's damn terrifying.

The National Institute of Mental Health provided the information below, and I sent it to Cam's teachers and our closest family and friends when we received the diagnosis.

It explains the many ways that a child can be impacted as well as a variety of resources to seek treatment.

For those of you who need the most important information *right now*, here you go:

*What is PANDAS?* *PANDAS is short for Pediatric Autoimmune Neuropsychiatric Disorders Associated with Streptococcal Infections. A child may be diagnosed with PANDAS when: Obsessive-compulsive disorder (OCD), tic disorder, or both suddenly appear following a streptococcal (strep) infection, such as strep throat or scarlet fever. The symptoms of OCD or tic symptoms suddenly become worse following a strep infection. The symptoms are usually dramatic, happen "overnight and out of the blue," and can include motor or vocal tics or both and obsessions, compulsions, or both. In addition to these symptoms, children may become moody or irritable, experience anxiety attacks, or show concerns about separating from parents or loved ones.*

*What causes PANDAS?* *Strep bacteria are very ancient organisms that survive in the human host by hiding from the immune system as long as possible. They hide themselves by putting molecules on their cell wall so that they look nearly identical to molecules found on the child's heart, joints, skin, and brain tissues. This hiding is called "molecular mimicry" and allows the strep bacteria to evade detection for a long time. However, the molecules on the strep bacteria are eventually recognized as foreign to the body and the child's immune system reacts to the molecules by producing antibodies. Because of the molecular mimicry by the bacteria, the immune system reacts not only to the strep molecules but also to the human host molecules that were mimicked; antibodies "attack" the mimicked molecules in the child's own tissues. These antibodies that react to both the molecules on the strep bacteria and to similar molecules found on other parts of the body are an example of "cross-reactive" antibodies. Studies at the National Institute of Mental Health (NIMH) and elsewhere have shown that some cross-reactive antibodies target the brain—causing OCD, tics, and the other neuropsychiatric symptoms of PANDAS."* **Are there any other symptoms associated with PANDAS episodes?** *Yes. Children with PANDAS often experience one or more of the following symptoms in conjunction with their OCD or tic disorder:*

- *Symptoms of attention-deficit/hyperactivity disorder (ADHD), such as hyperactivity, inattention, or fidgeting*

- *Separation anxiety (e.g., child is "clingy" and has difficulty separating from his or her caregivers; for example, the child may not want to be in a different room in thehouse from his or her parents)*

- *Mood changes, such as irritability, sadness, or emotional lability (i.e., tendency to laugh or cry unexpectedly at what might seem the wrong moment)*

- *Trouble sleeping*

- *Nighttime bed-wetting, frequent daytime urination, or both*

- *Changes in motor skills, such as changes in handwriting*

- *Joint pains*

It's horrifying and some next-level sci-fi shit. Except that it's very real.

Our pediatrician helped us contact the team at UT Southwestern and Children's Health in Dallas, who are the leading clinical experts treating PANDAS in our region. The team reviewed Cam's records and asked us to come in for an intake appointment.

We didn't know what to expect, but we went to Dallas. I was terrified that we would face this panel of experts who would look at us like we were out of our minds. Halfway through the 5-hour marathon appointment, during which we met with seven specialists, I burst into tears. I felt silly and explained that I didn't understand why no one was flinching when I explained what I knew must sound crazy.

The clinician leading the research at UT Southwestern replied, "None of what you've described sounds crazy to us, and this isn't the first time we've heard it."

That took my breath away.

And then it got even better. There were treatment options! Not only did they want us to take part in a genetic study of autism, they were also doing a gut-biome study and wanted to include Cam in that as well. They explained the current treatment options for PANDAS. IVIG (intravenous immunoglobulin) and fecal transplantation were discussed. They offered to connect us to a family whose child's medical profile was nearly identical to Cam's and has experienced incredible therapeutic results.

I wish I could explain the weight that was lifted off my shoulders that day.

Cam was a trooper through all of their tests, interviews, and examinations, and then he had a very thorough panel of blood work drawn and, lastly, an EEG.

We left for Thanksgiving break, and it unburdened my heart. Toward the end of our vacation, we noticed a surge in OCD behaviors, tics (including a loud squeaking noise), and this time some intrusive thoughts at such a rapid rate that I didn't doubt what we were seeing. We took a trip to the urgent care clinic (they know us pretty well by now!) and Cam had his throat swabbed again. Strep positive.

Today, Cam is on his fourth round of antibiotics since August. Only because this damn infection is insidious and resistant, not because we want this for him. Even though there are obvious benefits to each round, there are also significant risks associated with antibiotic use. His gut is receiving the highest-quality non-histamine-inducing probiotics available, as well as restorative supplements that help him recover from antibiotic use. Who knows how long Cam has carried the strep in his body? Who knows what it will take to eradicate it?

So why not just remove his tonsils and adenoids? That isn't a viable option for him at this point. The infection hides and lies dormant because it engages in molecular mimicry. It can remain undetected elsewhere in the body, so for children with PANDAS, it takes a different approach.

This time, we could get a longer dose of an antibiotic, hoping we can finally beat the strep infection and move onto the next phase of the treatment protocol once it is behind us.

The hope lies in the knowledge we are gaining from this very collaborative and scientific approach to all that is Cam.

The challenge is chasing down the therapies that are successful in treating PANDAS but aren't covered by insurance or readily available. Thankfully, more and more researchers and clinicians are successfully treating PANDAS and other types of autoimmune brain disorders.

Children with PANDAS can experience complete recovery.

Complete recovery.

This is not true of autism, and we have no desire to change who he is, but helping Cam maneuver his journey in a way that allows him to live his best life is what it is all about. Since the more obvious symptoms of PANDAS became prominent this summer, Cam has become acutely aware of the things that are outside of his control.

Just yesterday, on the way to school, he asked me, "Mama, do you want to know how I feel?"

Thinking that he was referring to strep throat, I responded, "Of course I do. How do you feel?"

He answered, "Do you want to ask me about the squeaking? About turning my head? Do you want to ask me?"

So, I took a deep breath and asked. "How do you feel about those things, Cam?"

He looked out the car window and said, "It bothers me a lot."

I took another deep breath and reminded him that Rob and I loved everything about him.

My prayer is that the clouds will clear again. Hopefully, this time, forever.

—·—

## ADVENTURES OF CAM & ALEXA

### DECEMBER 7, 2019

T here are days when I have to laugh out loud at the regular absurdities that exist within our day-to-day lives. Mostly, it *is* a rather funny adventure that we're on. Cam recently realized that our Alexa device is rather useful if you know the right questions to ask, and boy does he have a lot of questions. While I was cleaning the kitchen, the following conversation took place:

Cam: Alexa! Tell me about M&M's.

Alexa: Shuffling songs by Eminem

*("Not Afraid," began to play, and I felt fairly certain there weren't any words to be concerned about. I giggled to myself remembering my days of working at Interscope.)*

Cam: (annoyed) Alexa, stop! No! Tell me about M&M's!

Alexa: Shuffling songs by Eminem

*("Lose Yourself" began to play, and I quickly scanned through the lyrics in my memory. Okay, still safe.)*

Cam: (Getting very frustrated) Alexa, stop! No! Listen to me, Alexa! Tell me about M&M's!"

Alexa: Shuffling songs by Eminem

*(As the intro to "The Real Slim Shady" began to play, I immediately turned and screamed at the countertop device!)*

Me: ALEXA STOP!

Phew! That was a close call. My life sure has changed in 15 years.

— • —

# Music is Therapy

## January 6, 2020

I was working at home this evening when Cam came downstairs with his guitar and a piece of paper that had the lyrics from his favorite song written on it. You know, the one from *Snoopy! The Musical*. He asked me to grab my phone and record a video, so I did.

This has *never* happened before.

Cam usually refuses to sing, and, to be honest, he asks me to stop singing several times a day.

Afterward, he erupted into applause, cheering for himself at the top of his lungs, with a raucous, dramatic, and drawn out, "Wooooo hooooo!"

Then he promptly said, "Mama! I made a song! Put me on your playlist!"

I'm sharing this hoping you, too, will see the beauty, humor, and magic in a little boy whose heart has found joy in singing the words, "If just one person believes in you..."

## 34 Urinals

### February 1, 2020

G uess who tested positive for strep this week? We can't seem to slay this beast. But, we are readying ourselves for a more aggressive approach and waiting on the decisions of our medical team. Luckily, we caught this flare before it got too intense, and he's already improving both physically and neurologically. This is the 5th and strongest round of antibiotics that he has had to endure since the beginning of the school year. Thankfully, we counter the effects of this through some strong anti-inflammatory probiotics and a blend of yeast-biotic so that we protect *and* heal his gut.

Before you offer advice: Unless you have experienced an autoimmune condition yourself, or are an expert in neurological conditions such as autoimmune encephalitis, please don't. If a therapeutic approach exists, we've probably already researched it and are considering it or we have eliminated it. PANDAS is so complicated and we are exploring every viable option.

Despite the challenges that he has been facing, Cam is rocking in almost every other area. He's progressing at school, making huge strides in his language acquisition, and of course, with his art. Recently, he's taken to creating clay critters that turned out amazing! He's quite talented and I love seeing the look of pride on his face as he unveils each new masterpiece.

He rediscovered an old issue of Texas Monthly and it made his entire morning. The cover featured an army of the beavers from Buc-ees, which is his favorite store. Mainly because they have a Dippin' Dots stand, and it's the traditional pit stop between our house and his grandparents! Did you know that the store off of 290 on the way to Houston has 34 urinals?

Yep. You're welcome.

Fun fact: He has been keeping a running record of the number of urinals in every place he's ever been. At first, I didn't believe he was accurate.

*Of course he was.*

Now... If I could just get him to apply that photographic memory to math facts!

—  ◆  —

# CONVERSATIONS FROM ANOTHER ROOM

## APRIL 7, 2020

I was working in the living room when Cam started a conversation through the wall, like he often does. It's one of those endearing things that is hard to correct because sometimes he simply needs downtime and wants to be by himself after a hard day of peopling. He often pings a thought or comment out into the abyss, as if he's echolocating to make sure we're still there if he needs us. And we always ping back.

Cam: Mama! I'm having netagive thoughts!

Me: (subtly correcting his pronunciation of the word) *Negative* thoughts? Oh, no! What do you think you should do?

Cam: Let it float away like a balloon! Me: That's right. Where are you?

Cam: I'm on the potty...

Me: Oh! OK, well, close your eyes and imagine the balloon. What color is it?

Cam: I don't know!

Me: Well, what color would make you happy?

Cam: Blue!

Me: OK! Perfect! Close your eyes, and imagine that blue balloon. Now think about that negative thought and put it inside the balloon. Take a big breath in and then blow that balloon and the negative thought away like the wind...

Cam: *blows a long exhale...* Bye-bye!

And all was right in Camelot, once again.

# A Work of Art

## April 10, 2020

I used to spend countless nights lying in bed, awake and worrying, wondering if the words would ever come.

Autism is a complicated disorder, affecting each individual differently. We knew the biggest issues for Cam were social skills and communication, so the bridge to connecting Cam to the world had to be made of words. Each year, we turned to countless hours of therapy services to build his skills.

Single word demands morphed into short phrases.

"Milk" became "I want milk" with constant practice and 24/7 repetition...

My husband and I often laughed, imagining the thoughts behind the confused and judgemental looks we received from passersby at the grocery store.

"Bapple!"

"Good job! Now, say APP-le."

(Repeat, repeat, repeat)

Strangers didn't understand why we perseverated over the precise pronunciation of the items going into our cart. To be perfectly honest, I gave up explaining or justifying my parenting decisions long ago. Mainly, I credit Brené Brown for this glorious gift. I discovered her work one month after Cam was born, and she's been a part of my imaginary brain trust ever since. Every book she's written has helped me to embrace my wholehearted self while I work to cultivate an authentic life. The following passage from her book, *Rising Strong*, has served as a constant reminder for me:

> *A lot of cheap seats in the arena are filled with people who never venture onto the floor. They just hurl mean-spirited criticisms and put-downs from a safe distance. The problem is, when we stop caring what people think and stop feeling hurt by cruelty, we lose our ability to connect. But when we're defined by what people think, we lose the courage to be vulnerable. Therefore, we need to be selective about the feedback we let into our lives. For me, if you're not in the arena getting your ass kicked, I'm not interested in your feedback.*
>
> -Brené Brown

Eventually, the short phrases became bona fide sentences.

"I wanna nuggle" became "Mama, can we have a snuggle?" Still following the same pattern of the acquisition of language for toddlers, but also very different for us because Cam was in kindergarten.

We were still so very far behind.

I say we, and not merely "he" because it is our journey and we walk through it every step of the way, together.

We held fast to the belief that although he was years behind his peers with verbal communication, if we just kept at it, building skill upon skill, like creating a masterpiece made of LEGO bricks, one day it would all come together. One day, a bin full of individual pieces will become a work of art.

It took Michelangelo years to paint the ceiling of the Sistine Chapel, right?

Some of his greatest lessons in language have come from learning and reenacting the scripts of his favorite movies. Once he's comfortable with the script, he adapts it into his own repertoire and eventually breaks apart the pieces, incorporating each one into his vocabulary. It's different, but it works. And we play along, engaging in scripts that are both comfortable and familiar. If you could see the joy that it brings him in those moments, you would understand completely.

You haven't really lived until you've had an argument with your child in full character from a Disney Pixar movie.

Once he learned to read, it was a different ballgame. Just last week, he came bursting into my office, wide-eyed and breathless, to ask me what the word "catastrophic" meant. He became completely enamored with this word and has been using it to describe everything ever since. Apropos, I suppose.

As difficult as it has been trying to juggle our full-time work and parenting responsibilities with the added weight of teaching fourth grade curriculum during a global pandemic, it has also given us the opportunity to teach Cam in an intimate setting with guidance from his team. This week, we created science experiments, conquered math assignments, and brainstormed ideas for a writing assignment that turned into something spectacular.

And the words? They're *all* in there. They may have been there all along, but needed a lot of love, creativity, and a unique approach to bring them out.

# BIG BOOK OF QUESTIONS

## SEPTEMBER 12, 2020

There's something magical happening at our house. Cam, typically a man-cub of very few words, has started asking questions with rapid-fire frequency. We've heard the full gamut this morning, from "What is love?" to "How is cheese made?" While most kids begin the relentless "why" stage when they're much younger, he started this only recently. Let me tell you how difficult it is to make up an answer when your kid knows better.

Since we want him to experience the intrinsic reward of learning new things and he loves to write in his journal, I created a book titled *Cameron's Big Book of Questions.* He got to pick the first question to be answered: What is art?

First, I asked him what he thought. Then I had him write those ideas down, and we searched for some kid-friendly facts and definitions. He was *so* into it! Then, we looked up the different types of art, and he wrote each one down. We talked about how he is an artist because he loves to do every single one! When he was done, I asked him what he wanted to do next.

"I want to paint space!"

And that's exactly what he's doing right now.

PS: I'm absolutely counting this as his elective hours for the week!

— • —

# Rethinking the Weekend

## December 21, 2020

As our son grew older, and gained independence, it was pretty easy to fall into the habit of expecting him to need the same sort of unstructured down time on the weekend that most people seek. Time to himself, time to unwind, but let's be honest! Time to just *be*. Once he was responsible enough to spend time on his own in another room, we gave him expectations for behavior but also the freedom to spend that time however he wanted to. If we only knew then what we know now...

As an adult, I've always struggled with downtime, because I'm not relaxed unless I'm productive.

I know. It's counterintuitive, but true.

It makes little sense to people who truly enjoy the act of boredom. I have spent *years* trying to be comfortable with that, but for me it's an almost impossible ask.

I *need* rest, but it has taken me an entire lifetime of intentionally practicing *how* to rest, for me to do it without crawling out of my skin. Busyness is my addiction, and it often comes at a steep cost. On any given Monday when I return to work, I sometimes feel the pangs of a weekend poorly spent as the exhaustion creeps in when I've barely begun my work week. Luckily, I've learned firsthand that self-care is absolutely about discovering what helps you to best care for and manage your own needs. For me, that means knocking things off my to-do list while creating intentional ways to enjoy activities that provide rejuvenation. It's a different formula for every person, and one that I really enjoy helping others to discover.

So, in my efforts to teach my child better self-care habits, I assumed that providing him with a weekend full of unstructured downtime would be enough for a 10-year-old to begin the practice of regular rest. Erroneously, I thought that this would be his best chance at learning self-care. Like most of our *Adventures in Camelot,* he taught us another invaluable lesson.

Every weekend, somewhere between the middle of the day on Saturday and Sunday, Cam's inner beast would come out. It wasn't predictable at first, and the heightened dysregulation we were witnessing was brand new to us as parents. The slightest thing would send him into a full-blown meltdown.

Before you equate a meltdown with a tantrum, please don't.

For anyone in meltdown mode, the brain completely blocks the ability to learn anything in that moment. The simplest of things can trigger this for a child on the spectrum. The sound of an automatic hand dryer used to send ours into a frenzy that would be impossible to handle without an arsenal of well-practiced strategies. Usually related to some sort of sensory overload, Cam's meltdowns are very rare these days. In fact, the only time we witness this level of emotional dysregulation is when he is about to become very sick. It's only in hindsight that we can understand that his meltdowns usually predicate a serious fever or trip to urgent care. That was the case until a few weekends in a row of unstructured downtime!

The new behaviors were often so unpredictable that they would leave me reeling, searching for a cause that was no place to be found.

Until the day that I came across a post by one of my favorite autistic adult authors, Alis Rowe. She founded "The Curly Hair Project," which is *"a social enterprise that supports people on the autistic spectrum and the people around them..."* On Facebook, I follow her as The Girl with the Curly Hair! The insight provided by autistic individuals has frequently been the best learning experience for me as a neurotypical parent! One weekend, as I sat contemplating another meltdown that I didn't see coming, I saw one post from The Girl with the Curly Hair account that read, *"I always need to be 'doing' something. Empty time, unstructured time, even 'relaxing' time needs to contain an activity." - Alis Rowe*

Oh. My. Goodness.

It made perfect sense! Here I was, trying to create a restful environment for my child, and it was actually causing him distress! It was almost laughable... Except that it had been so exhausting for us both; it wasn't funny at all.

So, I called Cam down and I asked him which he preferred; time on the weekends to relax and do nothing or time filled with things to do. Guess what his answer was?

I sat down and started brainstorming ways to fill his weekend hours with an intentional scheduling of things that he finds highly enjoyable and also that challenge him, pushing him out of his comfort zone. The only thing worse than an anxious Cam is a bored one. I asked him what kinds of things we should include in his schedule and we built his schedule, together, from there.

The new schedule started after breakfast and filled up the hours of his day until bedtime. While his weekdays already have a very regimented schedule to help to accommodate his homeschooling hours, as well as ways to keep himself busy and safely occupied so that my husband and I could work remotely, weekends never had the same rhythm. This weekend, I put the schedule into place and saw his anxiety and dysregulation decrease drastically! He was back to the easygoing, snuggly kid that we know as Cam. I could see him physically settle into the relaxation of having activities that fulfilled him while knowing what to expect next. He had choices for each category, and that was a winning moment for both of us! For example, if it was creative time, he could choose between working with clay, drawing, coloring, painting, etc. If it was free time, he got to do *whatever* he wanted for that section of time. After he read a chapter of his book he could choose 30 minutes of screen time from making videos with his camera, playing video games, or watching TV. At the end of his day, he could settle in and watch a movie if he chose to.

While it's most definitely a work in progress, it's a start!

The shift in his behavior yesterday was abrupt and while it definitely took considerable effort, it was so worth it to see the level of peace it provided him. That's what it's all about, really. He is absolutely allowed to experience the frustration and emotional distress that life brings, and boy, does it bring those elements in waves these days. But, if I can empower him with the tools and strategies to help him maneuver this challenging world a little easier, then that's what I will always try to do. Every time.

For now, we will keep working on creative ways to help him thrive, even on the weekend, through intentionally structuring his days with scheduled breaks and activities that keep his mind and body fulfilled.

# It's Not Always Sunshine and Rainbows

## May 20, 2021

I have experienced people disappearing from our lives because autism was too much for them, or it didn't fit into their social landscape.

I have lost close friends when the invites stopped coming, because there's a lot I simply can't commit to, and sometimes I cancel plans at the last minute when Cam needs me to create an environment of calm and safety.

I've bent, and I have broken, trying to fit myself, our family and our child into events, trips, and traditions that made life much more comfortable for everyone else. What no one on the outside knows is that sometimes the simplest things take days or weeks of preparation and practice, and then leave us reeling in recovery mode for weeks after. No one is ever the wiser because I work myself into the ground trying to make it work.

I have experienced loved ones attempting to mask Cam's disability for their own convenience and comfort, dreaming of the day when he would be *just like all the other kids.*

This kid is a brilliant shining star. If you know and love him, then you know that he has always been destined to be different.

What I've learned through these experiences is that the friends and family who continue to show up, to celebrate the victories with us (no matter how small), and learn about autism without relying on us to educate them… They are the ones that matter.

So, if you're reading this, chances are you're one of those invaluable people in our lives who we couldn't possibly live without. You *are* #TeamCam, and I thank you for being our village, from the deepest part of my Mama Bear heart.

# BACK TO THE BIG APPLE

## JULY 1, 2021

E ight years ago, we moved to NYC to obtain the best early intervention services available at Cam's beloved preschool, QSAC (Quality Services for the Autism Community), which specializes in supporting individuals with autism. He still remembers every single adult and classmate from that time, and many of them are still very much a part of #TeamCam. The stories he tells us now from his experiences there when he was not yet communicating are so enlightening and a powerful testament to how supported he felt in that environment.

After a year and a half, we returned to Texas hoping that Cam would continue to make similar progress in elementary school. We had many influential teachers, so many wonderful experiences, and it was wonderful to be closer to my husband's family. However, the constant fight for adequate special education services was not sustainable.

This year, we took another giant leap of faith to ensure that Cam would have access to the best educational opportunities available, and we bought a house and some land in Upstate New York. After witnessing the budgeting and political bloodbath that was already at work within Texas public schools, we knew it would not improve the state of special education.

Rob and I made the painful choice to move again in pursuit of what we knew Cam needed: a quality education with layered special education support. We also knew that we could find these services in New York. We created a formula for what our family needed based on factors that were very important to us. And then we set to work, narrowing down our options until we decided where we wanted to create a home.

Cam is already *thriving*. Sometimes we don't know what the outcome will be, and the process is absolutely terrifying. There's a lot of sacrifice and discomfort, and I'll be honest, there are a lot of unknowns, which gives me significant anxiety. However, the risk is far less than the beautiful magnitude of the reward. We never make choices for our family without an incredible amount of research, and this one has left us feeling more confident than any choice we've ever made.

The sky's the limit, buddy.

# A Favor...

As I was walking by Cam's bedroom this afternoon, I overheard him happily chatting away. I paused to listen to what he was saying because he had been talking non-stop and he sounded different.

As I listened, I realized he was practicing intraverbals or social exchanges. Intraverbals comprise a lot of our day-to-day language, such as words, phrases, sentences, etc., that we use in response to another person's verbal communication. You know, in basic conversation, when one person makes a comment and another person responds to that comment in kind, and the flow seems both effortless and rewarding?

Well, social communication has always been so challenging for Cam. Over the years, he's put in a lot of effort to master this through explicit instruction and practicing skills 24/7. Words are simply not his native language.

He's a man-cub of very few words, and sometimes, although he has a lot to say, a situation can confuse him, and then his anxiety will often silence him.

If you're in his inner realm of trusted people, sometimes he never stops talking. However, the place that has always been so difficult for him to get a word in edge-wise was school. The setting where our earliest friendships are formed is often his greatest obstacle.

As I listened on the other side of the door, my Mama Bear heart broke a little.

"Oh, hi friend!"

"Are you sure?"

"Oh, I don't think so."

"No, thank you."

"That sounds good."

"That's very nice!"

"Would you like to play?"

It was such an intensely bittersweet moment because I realized in that moment that my son has much more self-awareness than I give him credit for. He sees the need to practice these skills. And he knows the role that he should play in the conversation.

However, he is probably growing acutely aware that the response time to respond to a classmate in order to connect with them is so fast. Hesitate, say the wrong thing, or spin your hands in the motion of a piston because you're nervous, and well, sometimes it's game over for that connection.

Or worse.

You guys... Puberty is approaching, and this stuff is getting so much harder. I can no longer go into his classes to teach his classmates about autism. He's too old for that. And I want him to experience autonomy and genuine friendship, no longer facilitated by his mama or his teachers.

This year is different, as many "new kid" challenges lie before us.

Cam has always been surrounded by amazingly cool classmates and kids. I credit this to the fact that he's had some outstanding teachers who really fostered an inclusive environment in their classes. And honestly, my kid is a rock star. I may be biased, but I think his friendship would be worth his weight in gold.

He's funny, better yet, he's silly.

He's so insanely creative! Clay, painting, drawing... These are his passions.

He's super knowledgeable about trains, and can actually drive (simulated) the Long Island Railroad thanks to his favorite video game, Train Sim World. He doesn't, however, drive it at a safe speed or bother to pick up the folks patiently waiting at Jamaica station as he flies by.

He's really into all things space and knows more about the solar system and NASA than most kids his age.

He loves with his whole heart, and he never asks for anything in return.

OK, maybe that's not true. His best bud, Riley, back in Texas, would say that Cam had to supervise *and* direct every aspect of railroad track construction that they engaged in. Riley's a very generous friend who sees Cam for who he is, and probably one of the first boys his age that accommodates the environment *for* Cam! Remember the *Little Girl at Recess?* Rayanna figured out early on that we build friendships through the work put in by both parties, and she's still very much a part of our lives. Coincidentally, I became good friends with the parents of both, and I can tell you they put great intention into raising exceptional humans.

The social hierarchies of the next few years are an almost impossible puzzle for typically developing children, but they are often a complete enigma for the neurodivergent. My entire being aches as I realize he will struggle, he may be hurt, and he will, inevitably, feel out of place. I so desperately want to shield him from this, but I know I can't.

This is where the favor comes in...

My request for you is that you take a few moments to have a conversation with the children in your lives about friendship and inclusion.

Remind them that every student in their class and school is worthy of feeling a sense of belonging in that space.

*There are no exceptions.*

Encourage them to seek friendships with all children, not merely as a nicety or some form of misguided charity, but because they, too, will benefit so much from it.

Remind them of how painful it can feel to be excluded and establish a dialogue that will help them feel comfortable coming to you or a teacher when they see another student being treated unkindly.

If they see someone sitting alone at lunch, suggest that they take the time to make sure they feel included. Get to know them. It takes so very little energy and the impact it may make is invaluable.

Learn, together, about the differences that make us unique, whether it's a disability, like autism, or any multitude of factors that could be a part of a child's identity.

I can not protect my son from all the unknowns of this social roller coaster that he's on, but together we can raise our children to be the compassionate, caring and inclusive friends that every child deserves.

And just maybe, if we do it often enough, it will ripple into Cam's world.

— • —

# Every Moment Matters

## November 21, 2021

In our world, teaching/practicing/coaching is a 24/7 gig that does not afford much down time. Every interaction is an opportunity for teaching and learning - for all of us. We do our best to model and repeat the skills that we hope Cam will gain, and always work to explain the ever elusive "why" that neurotypical individuals have set in stone for their own comfort.

Read that last sentence again.

The most profound lesson we have learned on this journey is radical acceptance. For Cam, for ourselves, and because we will always have to advocate fiercely to ensure that his needs are met. We will *never* try to shape Cam into something he is not.

The rest of y'all need to do better to accommodate neurodivergent individuals.

Some things take many attempts, failures, and tweaks in our approach, but it's how it works when you have an autistic child. There is no single approach, as every autistic individual differs from the next. We are big fans of a strengths-based approach with all things, and he is thriving as a result.

The three main areas that we focus a majority of our energy on are:

-Communication
-Social Skills
-Executive Functioning Skills

Lo-and-behold, this kid just showed us that all the practice we put into building his executive functioning skills is working! He hijacked the "meal menu" board for the week, and I ain't mad about it.

He wanted to plan out his week for the Holiday.

This is a BFD and I am 100% here for it.

# Let's Snuggle Up

## November 22, 2021

Last night after a marathon painting session, my cousin Alex took a picture of Cam and I that truly filled my heart. Cam had sidled up next to me and said, "Mama, let's snuggle up!" He crawled under the blankets with me and let out an enormous sigh, followed by, "There. I'm going to be just fine…" I love these precious and far too infrequent moments when Cam and I are simply at ease. Our world is so busy, and we work so hard.

Actually, let's give credit where it's due. *Cam works so hard.* In fact, he works harder than anyone I have ever known.

And to be honest, I'm really hard on him.

A lifelong, dozen plus therapy hours per week, and teaching him integral skills 24/7 have instilled this in us as parents, because we know we are often the driving force behind his success.

I have high expectations for him because I've never witnessed something that he cannot do. With most skills or milestones, we measure things in *Cam time.* When he's damn good and ready… Boom! Mastery.

Recently I've been reflecting about how much harder he has to work than most of his peers to accomplish the same basic tasks but while doing *so much more.*

At any given moment, he's giving everything he's got to gain new information with a completely different learning style than most teachers are comfortable with or possess even the most basic of training to address. He's tuning out distractions and learning to exist within the most unfriendly sensory environment in the world, and trying to translate rapid fire social cues into his own language of understanding in order to process a response of his own in the fraction of time that a neurotypical peer will wait for him.

Don't forget the pull-outs for services that he needs to progress. These happen within the school day, and while providers try to schedule these conveniently with the least impact to a child's schedule, it is a constant interruption to his attention, which he already struggles with. I am so thankful for his current school, where most of these services follow a *push in* model. Still, the amount of daily transitions is insane.

Speech Therapy
Reading/Writing
Science
Social Studies
Physical Therapy
Lunch
Occupational Therapy
Specials (art, music, PE, library, private percussion, etc.)
Math
Social Skills

It's important to note that the schedule of all the above changes every day, on a 6-day rotation.

When I have the time to reflect on how incredibly far he has come and on the daily progress he makes, I am left feeling completely in awe of him. Thanks for the picture, Alex. It reminds me to take many more opportunities to slow down, be still, and enjoy this time because it is heartbreakingly fleeting. My little boy is growing up, and with every day that passes, he is affording me fewer moments to "snuggle up."

# THE BIGGER PICTURE

## DECEMBER 17, 2021

Phew—it's been a week! Cam's teacher is an incredible collaborator. Today, she mentioned he's been quite distracted during independent work, often looking around the room. Because she knows about his struggles with PANDAS, she wanted to ensure I knew about this change right away. Of course, my mind started going to the places where fear, anxiety, and despair lie in wait, ready to send me spinning.

Tonight, as Cam was working with clay at the kitchen table, his twitching fingers caught my attention. As he was talking, he held his hand under the table, and I saw it was still moving. I suspected he had developed a new tic, so I asked him to show me his hands, and he opened them up, displaying that they were empty.

I asked him, "What are you doing with your hands, buddy?"

He replied, defensively, "I'm not doing anything!"

I knelt down and placed my hand on his knee. "It's okay, Cam. You can tell me. There's nothing to be ashamed of."

"I'm just doing the alphabet, Mommy."

The train of thought I was on made a screeching stop, so I asked him to show me.

He lifted his right hand and rolled right through the ASL alphabet.

I was so shocked and impressed—I let out a joyful laugh and asked, "Where did you learn this?"

"In Mrs. M's classroom!"

I emailed his teacher, who confirmed there *are* posters of the ASL alphabet on her classroom walls, which circle the entire room. When she realized that the reason he was looking all over the room was because he had taught himself using those images, she replied, "Of course he did!" She, too, was over the moon when he showed her what he'd taught himself over the past few days.

That's our Cam, always reminding us to see the bigger picture.

# SIMPLIFY

## DECEMBER 13, 2022

I'm establishing an intention for the upcoming year. My "one word," my mission?

SIMPLIFY

I don't believe resolutions are effective. In order for lasting behavior change to occur, it takes deep and intentional thought (and analysis) coupled with a plan of action and motivation. And the reward for making that change *must* be greater than the previous behavior (sometimes merely doing nothing to address a needed change) in order to stay motivated.

FROM SURVIVING TO THRIVING

Our family life is messy and complicated, albeit uniquely beautiful and precious at the same time. Parenting a child with complicated needs adds layers of complexities that are hard to understand unless you're in the middle of it yourself. I can't tell you how many times I've tried to emphasize this to those who matter only for them to respond, "But you make it look so easy." Multiple therapies a week, music lessons to build upon strengths, hours of homework, creating social opportunities, exposure to as much of the world as is possible and 24/7 teaching of skills.

If you're a part of our inner circle, you know this to be true, even though we often work ourselves into the ground to ensure that it all goes off without a hitch.

The problem with this is that it isn't sustainable. Juggling all the things while working full time creates a dynamic that is detrimental to any person and their family. I give 100% to everything I do, 100% of the time. What I've recently learned is that because folks know this about me, they rely on me to get shit done. Unfortunately, this also means that I am frequently the person who they turn to when they want or need their load lightened. For the first time in my life, I'm unapologetically pushing back on this expectation from others. There's quite a contradiction in knowing that your heart's purpose is to serve others, but also recognizing that you cannot pour from an empty cup.

GRACE

A few years ago, my mentor asked me how I could find all the Grace for the young people that I served, but none for myself. It stuck with me. So much, in fact, that the word "Grace" became an integral part of a lifelong healing process in dealing with my own traumatic youth. There's a plaque upon our mantle that simply reads, "Grace." It is my reminder that I, too, deserve all the Grace in the world. I cannot carry the weight of the world, not even the weight of our small world, entirely on my own. It's simply too heavy.

The problem is that there is absolutely nothing pertaining to the needs of my child that I will let fall to the wayside. Therapies? Nope. Music lessons? Definitely not. Ensuring his opportunities for a quality education? Not on my watch. Never gonna happen.

So, recently I began taking each aspect of my life through the paces of determining what is integral and what is not. Social Media is one place I could feel my energy being depleted almost every time I engaged. A few weeks ago, I deleted Twitter and never felt a single pang of regret. I guess I simply realized that one of my favorite sources of professional development (I follow a lot of folks in similar industries who inspire and educate me) had lost its value. I deleted another account for the same reason. It felt like an obligation to engage. This trend continues, although I do not know where it will lead. This was the easiest change to implement right away. As I evaluated the areas of my life that no longer served me, more things became apparent.

What areas of your life no longer serve you? Do you consciously choose to repeat the cycles that may harm you, or are they so well hidden behind good intention and chaos that you've never taken the time?

I highly recommend it.

## MANIFESTING PEACE

Even changing up my office space was an absolute game changer! When I transitioned to my hybrid role with the University, I made do by setting up shop in a corner of the downstairs where the man-cub has taken over; a cub cave if you will. Looking at my life with a mindful approach helped to shine a spotlight on my work space as an obstacle to establishing peace throughout my day. Multiple days of feeling chaos will yield to an abounding supply of stress, my friends. Multiply that by a decade or so...

I made the choice to move my office into the downstairs guest suite, and this simple move might have been the ultimate power play. I now have a space that is my own, and am enjoying decorating it with art that gives me joy, and creating a peaceful Zen den that I can retreat to for work, meditation, and yoga. The husband has his office upstairs, the man-cub has his own room and the entire downstairs as his own. Establishing my own sacred space was something that felt like a nicety until I realized it was a necessity. If you can make this happen in your space, it's so rewarding.

## ON SAYING NO

Have you ever noticed that the people who become upset when you establish a boundary are the exact folks who never respected them in the first place? I'm a natural people pleaser, not because I need folks to like me, but because serving others is truly my love language. I am completely fulfilled by helping people to become the best version of themselves. However, it often comes at a cost. As I draw lines in the sand, establishing boundaries that support my own mental and physical health, I am constantly surprised at how little care or compassion is returned from those who feel inconvenienced by it. This, too, is a lesson and boy am I learning.

SIMPLIFY

All of this leads me back to the goal of simplifying my life. 2023 holds a world of promise for our family, and each of us individually. The man-cub is learning to maneuver middle school, although we have had a bumpy ride. He's discovering his strengths and has also become hyper aware of his own shortcomings. My husband and I are both enjoying extremely rewarding careers that challenge us and also provide a lot of flexibility to manage the massive load of our family's needs. We still feel like we are juggling more than we should, but it no longer feels like the balls are on fire. And that, I suppose, is a start...

# It Wasn't Ever About the Duck

## April 4, 2023

L  ast summer, after a whirlwind weekend trip to Long Island, Cam realized he had lost his first stuffed animal. One that I bought off an end cap in Target out of sheer desperation. When he was an infant, he would grab for anything during a diaper change, so he needed something to hold and play with while we took care of business. The tiny terrycloth lovey became known as Changey Duck. In fact, I believe those words were two of his first before the regression began.

Fast forward 12 years to a loss of epic proportions. Not a single day has gone by since losing Changey Duck when Cam hasn't openly mourned his loss.

"Where did I lose him?"

"Is he all alone?"

"Did he fly away to a pond?"

"Do you think a little boy or girl has him?"

"Is he scared?"

Some might think that it was just a toy; he'll get over it! Folks, let me just explain that it was *not* the case. We held memorials, and Cam drew pictures that we framed and hung in Changey Duck's honor. Every night, Cam looped back into his worries and fears about his first friend.

On World Autism Awareness Day, while the boys were at art class, I tackled the linen closet located inside Cam's bathroom. Things had gotten quite messy as sheets, blankets, and towels were shoved in and pulled out by a well-meaning 12-year-old boy.

I shook out a fitted sheet I had bought for Cam's bed last summer and laughed, remembering how much he *did not* approve of its texture. His cotton star-patterned sheets have been a staple on his bed since he was 3, but these new sheets were a poly blend, and he simply wasn't having it. I can't say I blame him. If something doesn't feel right on your skin, it would be awful to sleep on it!

As I shook out the sheet to refold it, my main man, Changey Duck, tumbled to the ground.

I squealed.

I gasped.

I squeezed that little duck so tightly and then let out a full-throated, guttural, ugly cry.

You see, it wasn't ever about the duck.

The duck disappeared suddenly and without explanation, setting everything Cam knew to be true about the world into an out-of-control spin. But a few years ago, the same was true of Cam's grandfather. After suffering from a severe TBI and years of Cam (and everyone, really) trying unsuccessfully to connect once again to one of his favorite humans, he loaded a U-Haul with his belongings and disappeared from Cam's life entirely, without so much as a goodbye.

It wrecked him. His grandfather's inexplicable disappearance wounded Cameron like nothing I've ever witnessed. He, too, became different. He developed pretty severe anxiety and OCD with uncontrollable compulsions, and as hard as he tried, he could not make sense of the world anymore. As hard as we tried, we couldn't help him do that. Hundreds of therapy hours later, the duck disappeared, too, and it knocked our world off its axis once again.

*It wasn't ever about the duck.*

It was about the world ceasing to make sense and trying to regain his understanding of everything that he knew to be true. I've been there. You've probably been there. As a collective society, we *are* there. Together. We have witnessed the suffering when connections are severed. This week, I am so grateful for one loss to heal. With time, maybe the other will as well.

The information below is an excerpt from Bill Nason's Autism Discussion Page on Facebook that he has generously allowed me to include for context. Nason is an autism specialist and psychologist who has authored several books that I've added to my toolbox. Five out of five stars—would definitely recommend.

### Objects versus People

*Although it is a broad generalization, some children with autism have a greater interest and attention for objects, patterns, and concrete events (e.g., video games) then they do for people. Children will sit for hours engaged in solitary play with objects, with little awareness of what is going on around them. This, of course, is a generalization, with some children showing very high interest in people. However, for those with little social interest, the parents are often left feeling emotionally rejected and heartbroken that their children may never learn to enjoy relating with others.*

*First, let's look at why there is a strong interest in objects. One of the strong reasons may be that objects are concrete and predictable. Because of the children's inability to predictably read the actions of people, often misinterpret and react negatively, and get chastised frequently, interacting with people is unpredictable, confusing, and scary. This often creates strong social anxiety. Objects, sensory patterns (which they are attracted to) and concrete games are predictable, reliable, and the children feel competent since they can control them. Whether it is spinning a top, lining up cars, learning everything there is to know about trains, or mastering the next new video game; these events represent familiarity, predictability, and a sense of control. The social world is simply too chaotic and confusing for them.*

-Bill Nason

Ain't that the truth?

—·—

# LESSONS I'VE LEARNED

## APRIL 12, 2023

T his is a forever job. Because I'm still learning every single day, it would be impossible to pass it all on. Our on-the-job training provides limitless opportunities. However, I want to share the most important lessons that I've gleaned from parenting an exceptional child, hoping it will help even one person feel a little less afraid or alone.

## WORDS MATTER

This is your friendly reminder to be mindful of how you refer to individuals with disabilities. It will, and should, take you a bit of fumbling to figure it out. Words matter *greatly,* and when we get them wrong, it's so easy to fix them and move forward. When in doubt, ask. And when teaching others about the importance of using appropriate terminology, be sure to *teach from a place of love.*

Examples:

1. I'm the mother of a child with autism. I don't personally identify as an autism mom. I do identify as a woman, a New Yorker, a mom, a fierce advocate, and as neurodivergent. I don't criticize others for the labels they use for themselves or their children, unless they're harmful.

2. I often describe myself as the parent of a child *with autism,* because for right now, Cam has said that is how he prefers that language to be used. The minute he decides otherwise, I will change it to respect his wishes.

I use the word *autistic* at home and in my writing. I've gained a lot from listening to the autistic community, and I am always learning from them.

3. When I discuss the autistic community, you'll see that I frame my words differently because that is how the community (as a larger entity) has expressed how they wish to be identified.

This is also why I blend my use of the wording around Cam and in my writing, because normalizing the phrasing is vital, and neither *autism* nor *autistic* are words that should be associated with shame or embarrassment.

4. If someone mentions their disability in passing, I pay close attention to how they're phrasing it, and I change my words to mirror their own. Sometimes I ask clarifying questions to honor who they are so that I can be sure to get it right. *If you're reading this and it reminds you to respect other people's pronouns, yes! Exactly!*

5. If a person hasn't disclosed a disability, personally, it's not your place to label or diagnose them. Period.

It's simple. It's also complicated. *But it's always steeped in respect.*


## I'VE GOTTEN COMFORTABLE WITH GETTING THINGS WRONG

When this journey started, I relied a lot on the advice of professionals. "Your child needs eleventy million hours of multiple therapies each week in order to make him indistinguishable from his peers."

No.

Since you've already read through some of my most vulnerable moments of the last decade, I feel like I can be honest with you.

Take the therapy recommendations with a grain of salt, but focus your efforts on raising a tiny human who knows that...

- They are loved for exactly who they are.

- You will become a gladiator to fight any obstacle that stands in their way.

- You will empower them with the skills to do it themselves when they're ready.

- They are seen, heard, and valued for who they are. *Exactly* as they are.

- We are *all* a work in progress.

- You will always take a strengths-based approach to helping them discover their superpowers.

- They will accomplish greatness, no matter what deficits they may have.

Listen to the professionals, yes. *But also listen to your gut.* If it's possible, find adults who share the same disability as your child. Learn from them. Even (and especially) when it's uncomfortable.

## YOUR TEAM

Work to build a team. You will be the person who creates collaboration where there could be conflict. You will probably be the one with the eagle-eye perspective on all things related to your child. It will fall on you to connect the dots in order for the entire team to see the big picture. It will be both exhausting and invigorating, but please believe me when I say that you cannot do it all, nor should you be expected to.

It will take discomfort, pushing yourself beyond what you ever knew you were capable of, and immense trust.

Sometimes it will work to your benefit, and sometimes you will need to deconstruct your team.

I fired the first person who was assigned to our team because she violated one pillar of our core beliefs relating to the care of and goals for our son. She asked me what my goals were for Cam, and I explained I wanted him to connect to the world around him like he does with those who know him best. She scoffed at me and said, "Well, now you're talking out of both sides of your mouth. Is he connecting, or isn't he?"

I showed her to the door and reported the behavior to her supervisor. No one should ever attempt to demean or disrespect you or your child for any reason. Our teams should be collaborative and everyone must truly value the contributions of every member. It's okay to set this expectation up front.

After that day, I was vigilant regarding the expectations that I had set for anyone working with Cam. I made sure that I was crystal clear in relaying my expectations to every single provider who joined our team.


## SELF-CARE IS NOT AN OPTION

I understand how frustrating it is to realize that your days are full, you have negative bandwidth, you're exhausted, and everyone's telling you that "you really need to take time for yourself."

I've had this exact discussion with so many parents who struggle to find time for themselves. But let me be the first (or hopefully the last) to tell you:

***No one*** *is going to carve out the time for you or make it easier to achieve any modicum of self-care.*

It used to infuriate me when people would suggest it, and eventually I became completely depleted and suffered from caregiver burnout. I wasn't sleeping. My adrenals were shot. I had brain fog and became overly emotional. I had to change our entire schedule, and if I'm being honest, my life, to ensure that I could meet my own needs. After putting the man-cub first for 12 years, I finally figured it out, although it is definitely still a work in progress.

My best tips?

*Sleep.* You need it. However, you can achieve it in whatever way works for you, as long as you make sleep a priority. If you're struggling with sleep, I highly recommend making this your first big goal. If you're not sleeping well, nothing else feels right, and stress will feel heightened.

*Exercise.* Move your body. It helps to process emotions, improves your mental health, and is an amazing way to improve your sleep! Find a form that you enjoy, or at least one that you do not hate.

*Eat healthy foods.* Nourish your body. Eat nutritious foods and stay hydrated. Yeah, to any other crowd, I wouldn't preach to drink more water, but I know how it goes.

*Listen to your inner voice.* Sometimes self-care means conquering your to-do list, cleaning up your house, or staring at the wall. There is more to life than massages and pedicures, so find what feels good.

*Therapy.* None of us can process all of this alone, and caregivers need a champion to help process all the tumultuous emotions that we go through daily. Find a quality therapist that works with your schedule and, if possible, a support group for caregivers!

*Find your people!* Making friends as an adult parent is harder than I imagined, but as the parent of a child that is atypical, wow! So difficult. Find other parents who "get it," and support each other through the process. And when you do, start your own BAMs chapter. Dads, you are free to become the BADs.

*Marriage/Relationships.* If you have a partner, find intentional ways to strengthen and support your relationship. It is so easy to lose yourself in the ebb and flow of co-parenting a complicated child. One of the best things we've ever done is set up a weekly meeting to touch base and discuss what we need from each other, what's going well, and what we need to work on.

And for the first time in a very long time, we are trying to schedule a regular date night.

*Learn.* There are so many amazing resources available if you know where to look. Groups on social media offer a lot of opportunities for education. However, this can often feel like drinking water from a fire hose, so go easy on yourself. Don't go down the rabbit hole.

*Grace.* If there's any advice that I can give that you truly absorb to the core, let it be this: Give yourself the grace necessary to endure a lot of getting things wrong, not feeling as if it's good enough, not knowing which step to take next, or if it is the right one. You *will* mess up, fall apart, and inevitably find yourself face down in the muck of life's most challenging times.

Dust yourself off and try again. In fact, if I've successfully taught Cam anything, it's that mistakes are often how we learn and grow. One of my favorite things about learning alongside my son is when he reflects on our deep conversations. He always says, "I'll try again."

Like I told you, even when it feels like I'm teaching, I'm always learning.

# Dear Cameron

## April 13, 2023

When I started writing this story—our story—I had just learned that I was going to be a mother.

From the very first moment, I loved you beyond measure. I hope that if you ever read this, you will feel my deep love and admiration for you and who you are becoming. But mostly, I hope you will see how much you inspire me to be the best version of myself.

You have been my life's greatest teacher, and you will be my life's greatest legacy.

*My magnum opus.*

Everything that I put into raising you has come back to me a thousand times over. The joy that you have brought into my life is nothing short of magical. To watch you create art and music is to witness brilliance at a level that I can not adequately describe. Watching you learn skills and master them at a different pace than your peers is no longer painful because now I can see outside of myself and the arbitrary milestones that I once thought made sense. To this day, I have never witnessed something that you cannot do, given time.

I remember one of the first truly meaningful questions you asked me.

*"Mama, what is your most favorite thing?"*

I immediately answered, *"You,"* and this has been my truth since the moment I knew I was going to be your mother.

I love you, and I am so proud of who you are, all that you are becoming, and the hard work that you put into everything you do.

Let no one tell you what you cannot achieve, because you have already moved mountains, sweet boy.

Thank you for guiding me through these gloriously beautiful *Adventures in Camelot.*

♡ Mama

—   •   —

# Once Upon a Time

## Today

*O nce upon a time, a young boy embarked on a unique and often challenging journey. On his path, he met a team of dedicated educators and providers who believed that he was capable of greatness. Local village lore would have you convinced that his mother often took the shape of a fierce bear when provoked and that she was the catalyst for his transformation. She knew firsthand that the power and love of a village could surpass all odds, so she set out carefully, crafting a team of loving warriors who believed in diversity, equity, and inclusion. But in the end, it was the young boy who lifted the sword from the stone and removed all the obstacles from the path—his own damn self.*

*Educators,* above all else, continue to love and respect your students. Welcome meaningful collaboration with their families. Lean in, listen, and learn. Especially when it's uncomfortable.

*Parents,* support your children's educators, but also hold them and the systems that they work within accountable. When teaching is necessary, do it from a place of love. Help to paint a picture of your child's potential and empower them with the tools that you know are invaluable.

Trust, collaboration, and grace are the ingredients for success. Build your team carefully, because that success truly requires a village.

*The End*

# ACKNOWLEDGMENTS

## Gratitude Roll Call

Rob,
*Thank you for holding me steady in times when I questioned my strength.
And for the art that holds these precious pages of our journey together.
I love you endlessly.*

My beloved BAMs,
*Thank you for your love and support through the highest peaks and lowest
valleys.*

#TeamCam,
*Our beloved friends, family, and cheerleaders from afar—there aren't
adequate words to describe my gratitude. Thank you for being a constant
source of support and inspiration. We love you!*

**The following permissions were granted for use in this book:**

Autism Discussion Page. Objects versus People. *Facebook,* December 20, 2022, 5:22 am. https://www.facebook.com/autismdiscussionpage. Accessed April 4, 2023.

Coelho, Paulo., et al. *The Devil and Miss Prym: A Novel of Temptation.* 1st U.S. ed. New York, HarperCollins Publishers, 2006.

Excerpt(s) from RISING STRONG: THE RECKONING. THE RUMBLE. THE REVOLUTION. by Brené Brown, copyright © 2015 by Brené Brown, LLC. Used by permission of Spiegel & Grau, an imprint of Random House, a division of Penguin Random House LLC. All rights reserved.

The Girl With the Curly Hair. *Facebook,* December 10, 2020, 9:38 am. https://www.facebook.com/TheGirlWithTheCurlyHair. Accessed April 4, 2023.

JUST ONE PERSON (from the musical "Snoopy"). Lyrics by HAL HACKADY. Music by LARRY GROSSMAN. © 1976 (Renewed) UNICHAPPELL MUSIC, INC. All Rights Reserved. Used by Permission of ALFRED MUSIC.

Mellencamp, John. "Small Town." *Scarecrow.* PolyGram Records, Inc. 1985.

National Institute of Mental Health. (2019). PANDAS—Questions and Answers. (NIH Publication No. 19-MH-8092). U.S. Department of Health and Human Services, National Institutes of Health.

Rodakis, John. "An N=1 Case Report of a Child with Autism Improving on Antibiotics and a Father's Quest to Understand What It May Mean." *Microbial Ecology in Health and Disease,* vol. 26, no. 1, 2015, pp. 26382–26382, https://doi.org/10.3402/mehd.v26.26382.

"Our Children, Our Awakeners" from THE AWAKENED FAMILY: A REVOLUTION IN PARENTING by Shefali Tsabary, Ph.D., copyright © 2016 by Shefali Tsabary. Used by permission of Viking Books, an imprint